Headless Horus

The Dark Fated Tale of Arthur Rochford Manby

Arthur Rochford Manby on an afternoon trot along his grounds.
Photograph, Edith Kearny.

Headless In Taos

The Dark Fated Tale of Arthur Rochford Manby

James S. Peters

SUNSTONE
PRESS

SANTA FE

Other Works by James S. Peters

Mace Bowman: Texas Feudist, Western Lawman
(with Chuck Parsons)

Robert Clay Allison: Requiescat in Pace

Knight Errant: The Undoing of George Woods

Sunstone books may be purchased for educational, business, or sales promotional use.
For information please write: Special Markets Department, Sunstone Press,
P.O. Box 2321, Santa Fe, New Mexico 87504-2321.

Book and Cover design › Vicki Ahl
Body typeface › Adobe Jenson Pro
Printed on acid free paper

Library of Congress Cataloging-in-Publication Data

Peters, James Stephen.
     Headless in Taos : the dark fated tale of Arthur Rochford Manby / by James S. Peters.
          p. cm.
     ISBN 978-0-86534-735-9 (softcover : alk. paper)
     1. Manby, Arthur Rochford, 1859?-1929? 2. Swindlers and swindling--New Mexico--Taos--
Biography. 3. Taos (N.M.)--Biography. 4. Taos (N.M.)--History. I. Title.
     F802.T2P48 2010
     978.9'5304092--dc22
     [B]
                                        2009051830

WWW.SUNSTONEPRESS.COM
SUNSTONE PRESS / POST OFFICE BOX 2321 / SANTA FE, NM 87504-2321 /USA
(505) 988-4418 / ORDERS ONLY (800) 243-5644 / FAX (505) 988-1025

To Pete and Grace

"Taos, Thursday, July 4,
1929-A.R. Manby was
found dead at his house
on Wednesday morning
with his body in a mutilate
condition and his head
severed from his body."
—*Taos News*, July 4, 1929

Manby's Death in Taos

The sky was a bowl turned upside down
Above the earth reflector to the sun:
In the heat of noon the Indians walked
In winding blankets of haze locked
Through canyons where scrub cedar fought
The fringe of rock. Beneath that sun
Manby died of an axe struck,
Cleaving his throat, and the clot
Of his blood was dark on the rock.
      But his death was protected—
As his life had been. Manby was born
In silence, and his death seemed
The slow pulse of the earth beneath
Residual bone; over the glazed
Socket passed the hollow blaze
Of the sun. And the Indians moved
As the earth turned to the night,
Dark in the bowl of the sky
And black in Manby's face and mind.

—Norman Macleod
The New Mexico Quarterly
May, 1938, Vol. VII, Number 2

Foreword
by
Marc Simmons
from
The Santa Fe New Mexican
November 1, 2008

Arthur R. Manby of Taos was originally from England and a "remittance" man. This meant his family promised to provide him an annual income for life, provided he left the country and never returned. In plain fact, Manby was a black sheep.

What brought him to remote Taos in the first place is not exactly clear. In his early rambles, looking for an exile home, he must have heard that tiny Taos was accepting of eccentrics. At the time of his death in 1929, Manby occupied a sprawling adobe house on Pueblo Road. It had a large interior placita, or courtyard, and its stout outer walls had barred windows like a fort.

Daily, the occupant walked to the Taos plaza to shop and visit the post office. He regularly wore English riding pants, a floppy hat and a pistol belted at the waist.

Added to his menacing appearance, a large ugly dog followed him closely. Taos folk kept their distance. Rumors concerning the odd foreigner abounded. He was said to be involved in illegal land transactions and mining schemes.

On July 3, 1929, a U.S. deputy marshal appeared at the fortress-like residence to serve some kind of papers on Manby. He found the door locked and the windows tightly closed, even though the day was sweltering. No one answered his repeated knocks. The marshal's suspicions were aroused, and he summoned a deputy sheriff. That officer also became alarmed. So together the two lawmen climbed to the flat roof, walked to the edge of the placita and peered down.

They saw four large vicious dogs foaming at the mouth and barking wildly. It was evident they'd had no water for some days. The officers shot the animals. Then they dropped into the courtyard. After prying a door open, the pair gingerly entered the house. Manby's ugly dog and walking companion was found in the same condition as the four outside, and he, too, was shot. Next, the deputies discovered Manby himself lying on an army cot under a blanket, dead. His head, however, was missing.

That turned up shortly in an adjacent room; a bare skull with dog teeth marks on it was presumed to be that of Mr. Manby. The coroner on arrival decided that the man had succumbed in his sleep and had been dead for several days. The dog, becoming famished, must have chewed off his master's head and stripped the skull clean.

None of the Taos folk liked the grumpy old fellow, and may have thought him to be something of a wizard. Also, there was much speculation that he might have been murdered for his money. Plus, he had many known enemies scattered throughout the county.

Yet, there seemed to be no ready evidence of foul play. Hence, the coroner united the skull and body, and both were buried in the large garden outside the house. In time, the talk died away. Still, the belief grew up around town that it was bad luck to discuss the Manby death at all.

About 20 years ago, I was invited to a candlelight supper in Santa Fe. Attending were several other historians, including the late Dr. Myra Ellen Jenkins, who was then the state archivist and state historian. Around the dining table, illuminated by only two candles,

Jenkins told of giving a recent talk in Taos on the Manby case: As she got up to speak to the audience, the hall was shaken by a deafening clap of thunder and the lights went out.

It took 10 minutes or so to get them back on. After she spoke and was leaving, a local woman came up to her and declared seriously, "Mr. Manby's ghost doesn't like you talking about him." Jenkins dismissed the comment because her attention was focused on the heavy rain outside. With growing concern, she found her car in the dark and started the long drive south to Santa Fe.

As the highway began its twists and turns down into the canyon of the Rio Grande, the historian recalled: "Suddenly, my headlights quit on me. Unable to see, I went off the side of the road and came to a stop." She sat there a half-hour with the electrical system seemingly gone. Finally, she tried the starter again and the headlights magically came on. The drive to Santa Fe thereafter was uneventful.

As an eyewitness at the dinner, I can testify that, just as Jenkins finished relating her story, the two candles on our table sputtered out and we were left in the dark. Several diners gasped, while our host made it to the light switch and flipped it on. We looked at one another in astonishment and then laughed nervously at the "coincidence."

Surely it was merely that—but an uncanny coincidence, nonetheless. Or was it?

Preface

Arthur Rockford Manby was a driven man with the overwhelmingly ambitious dream of becoming a land baron, a vision he pursued for over thirty years. Arriving in Raton, New Mexico in 1883 from England, the twenty-three-year-old became exposed to the massive 1,714,764.94-acre Maxwell Land Grant of Colfax County which whet his appetite. It was the largest real estate swindle in the history of the southwest of 2,680 square miles, and at the time still being fought for in the courts. The grant company, with the corrupt political, legal and financial tactics of the Santa Fe Ring behind it, set the style for him, and in a small way he somewhat echoed their stratagem down the years.

After over three dogged decades of tenacious and persevering struggle, he finally won his place in the blazing sun of Midasean success with the ownership of the Martinez Grant of Taos, New Mexico. It encompassed nearly 100-square miles of acreage. Although minuscule when compared to the Maxwell, he felt he had arrived.

But alas, his victory was brief and crushing. As the old maxim describes, "Whom the Gods would destroy they first make mad." In his case the deities worked in reverse. After only three years in his possession, the grant slipped from his grasp. Then, a deeper and more tragic fate arrived to dog him inescapably, and the remaining years of his life was turned into a living hell.

—James S. Peters

Fate, lot, destiny, chance—
To which do we squirm, to
which do we dance?

                —Tasich

Part 1

Lachesis

Following the discovery of the decapitated corpse of Arthur Rochford Manby in his nineteen-room mansion in Taos, New Mexico, there quickly arose two schools of thought as to the event. One sect accepted he was gruesomely murdered, while the second held to the belief he had staged his death and left behind the cadaver of a stranger. The case was a bizarre enigma wrapped in riddles, confusion, betrayal and greed. Finally for posterity, and as relief to the guilty, it was labeled an unsolved crime. Today it is referred to as the "Manby Mystery of Taos."

To add to the already gristly drama, Manby's apparition, sometimes headless, was reported occasionally wandering the grounds of his old house. Frightened witnesses experienced a presence filled with vile intent and malevolence.

During Manby's residence in his newly adopted country of nearly fifty years he earned the disdain of many, and has been portrayed as a social pariah and a man of few principles. Many have labeled him a monster. Yet it is often overlooked that he was intelligent, educated and talented, and came from excellent family stock. Why he finally followed the profession of a confidence man is another part of the "Manby Mystery." Although his background was certainly above average academically and materially, the answer lies within the man alone and is buried with him. Whatever good or bad can be attributed to him, the distressing fact is that his story is a tale of human disintegration, the tragedy of a good mind destroyed, and as a result, talents miserably wasted.

According to an ancestor's chart drawn up by Manby, the family tree can be traced back several generations to Buckinghamshire

County, England and was festooned with the professions of Army, Navy, medical and religious personages. He lists his great-grandfather Edward as a "Surgeon, Royal Navy, Aide to Captain James Cook in the discovery of Australia in 1775." Boasting, he claimed Point Manby in southern Alaska was named for him.

His grandfather, the Reverend John Manby, was the fourth son of Dr. Edward and Judith Taylor Manby in a family of six. Prior to being ordained he was secretary to the Duke of Sussex, the third son of King George III. His position as Vicar of Lancaster was affirmed for him by the King, and a family heirloom is a gold watch from the ruler's son engraved, "To John Manby . . . from the Duke of Sussex."

Arthur's father, Edward Francis, was the last born of the Reverend John and Margaret Hamen Manby of a family of four. Edward was the rector at Morcambe, Lancashire and was "something of a country gentleman, a sporting and hunting parson, having a respectable amount of property and living on the lines of a country squire . . . . The family lived at Poulton Hall, and not in a vicarage residence . . . "

Arthur Rochford Manby was born 14 July 1859, in Morcambe to Edward and Emily Norton Manby, one of a brood of six boys and three girls. Arthur was the second-last child, and being his mother's favorite was said to have been dreadfully spoiled. Appointing herself his protector, she often took him on painting jaunts throughout the countryside, being an accomplished watercolorist. Mother and son would clamber into a horse-drawn cart with easel, canvas, and paints and trundle forth, stopping when a scene struck her fancy. For several hours she would paint her heart out, absorbed and happy, humming or singing softly at times, as Arthur stood entranced at the gradual appearance of a colorful rendition of the vision before them. It was magic to him, and he had to know how it was done. Soon he began grabbing a brush and daubing at her work as if to join her as a partner, sometimes smearing a corner of the picture. Instead of scolding him she would laugh and call him a struggling artist, gently take the brush from his hand and give him a peck on the nose.

Finally his insistence became an aggressive drive, so one morning she brought along an extra easel and canvas for him to daub upon. She was surprised at his enthusiasm, and thrilled at his budding talent as each canvas improved greatly over the last. It was a miracle to her and she encouraged and taught him all she could, which he drank up like a sponge. Learning the craft from her was a joy for him, and her paeans of praise over his intense efforts was nourishment to his starving soul. "Oh, that is so marvelous, Arthur! Such talent you have. I knew you were born to do fine things, Arthur. Yes, you are truly destined for greatness!" Her words of maternal acceptance and love were as honey to his heart, and those words clung to him as a second skin which he wore all his life.

As a youth he was of solitary turn, if somewhat dreamy-headed, and as he grew older he developed a burning need to make his mark, instilled assuredly by his mother. Educated in Belfast, Ireland, he ardently studied architecture, and later embraced a strong interest in mineralogy. In 1876, when Arthur was sixteen, his father passed away. His mother soon followed, and he was left desolate. At twenty, showing off to several junior siblings, he climbed the cement railing of the second floor balcony of their home. As he comically capered about, he slipped and plunged to the stone patio below. While physically surviving the fall, it was feared his head may have suffered damage, for the family noticed a change in him afterward. He became swift to anger and adverse to criticism; was often somewhat guarded and testy.

The exact dates or sequence of the arrival of the four Manby brothers, Alfred, Arthur, Charles, and Jocelyn, who eventually settled in America and Canada, is uncertain. But by mid-1883, all were fairly fixed in their new environment.

Charles, the oldest, had moved from their home in Morcambe to Birmingham, Worcestershire where he apprenticed himself as a chemist at a steel mill, and became a respected craftsman in his profession. He then crossed the Atlantic to live and remain in Pittsburgh, Pennsylvania where he worked in a mill of the rising steel magnate Andrew Carnegie, the "Dread Scott." Curious and inventive, family lore speaks of Charles inventing a chemical process pertaining to steel manufacture, but failing to patent it, lost it to the Carnegie Company.

Arthur, in May of 1883, claimed to have taken his share of the family's inheritance and sailed to the United States. His exodus had been strongly influenced after reading a glowing advertisement in a British newspaper describing the vast opportunities in ranching, farming, and mining on the Maxwell Grant. On 8 June 1883, the *Raton Comet* announced his arrival in Raton, New Mexico with two men, A.H. Hartley and E. Winter, "men of large means seeking ranches, ranges, and cattle to invest in." With this announced hyperbole, the nearly twenty-four-year-old assertive Arthur Rochford Manby, the dreamer of wondrous dreams, commenced his career as a self-proclaimed speculator and promoter of whatever appeared financially feasible. In short, he embarked in the trade of a confidence man.

By the time Arthur arrived in Colfax County, the Maxwell Land Grant was thirteen years into its battle for recognition. Originally a Mexican land grant of 97,000 acres, it was purchased in 1870 by speculators who resurveyed it to nearly two million acres. Over the ensuing years they would fight to legitimize their readjustment while mercilessly evicting the squatters, settlers, farmers, miners, and small ranchers as swiftly as possible. They naturally favored monied investors and big ranchers. One of the powers behind the grant was the Santa Fe Ring, a loose covey of politicians, lawyers, and financiers, and companion to the corrupt Republican party which held sway in the New Mexico Territory for thirty years. As a natural extension of his ethical evolution, the Ring and their methods became Arthur's *idee fixe*. But it was Colfax County's Frank Springer, arguing before the U.S. Supreme Court, who won on the side for the Maxwell Grant Company in 1887, legitimizing its size and scope. He was awarded 16,000 acres.

Jocelyn, the youngest of the quartet, had joined the British merchant marine, and the vessel he shipped out on had the chore of delivering wheat from Portland, Oregon to England via Cape Horn. During a storm off the coast of Chile he was washed overboard, but as the bobbing ship dipped into the violent sea again, he grabbed a line from the yardarm and hoisted himself back aboard. Because of damage suffered by the old sailing hulk, it returned to San Francisco for repairs. Jocelyn, having enough of sea duty, jumped ship there. Voluntarily returning to England under his own steam, he stood court-martial and was exonerated. In 1883, he joined Arthur in New Mexico. A short time later, Alfred purportedly followed. The three, Jocelyn, Arthur and Alfred, began ranching at Castle Rock in the upper Vermejo where they built their house.

As to the impression, and sometimes statements, that Arthur was a remittance man, it appears to have been utterly false and may have been one of his many fabrications in order to enhance his personal resume. Actually, at the disposition of the family estate after their father's death, the majority of the assets were invested undivided by the brothers and sisters. From this, the interest went to their sister, Mrs. Clara Athill, who was in poor financial circumstances due to her husband suffering a crippling heart attack. The estate was finally settled in June 1950, divided among some twenty-one heirs. It was felt Arthur borrowed heavily from Eardley, the oldest of the brothers who was a career officer in the British army. Perhaps from the occasional sums he received, probably extracted after seductive promises of rich returns via his chimeric land schemes, Arthur was able to give the desired impression of inherited wealth he habitually paraded. It has also been hinted he was the "black sheep," and was requested to vacate the family hearth.

Another creative fiction of Arthur's is the embellishment of his great-grandfather being a ship's surgeon with Captain James Cook, mentioned earlier, and of having Manby Point in southern Alaska named for him. On neither of the three Pacific cruises Cook made was there a medical man named Manby aboard any of his vessels, nor was Point Manby his namesake. An unrelated Thomas Manby, Master of the HMS Chatham on a later expedition, from 1791 to 1793, was bearer of the honor.

In 1884, Arthur and Jocelyn became involved in the shooting death of Daniel B. Griffin at their ranch, and the two faced charges of premeditated murder.

Following Arthur's purchase of four sections of land in Castle Rock from the Maxwell Land Grant Company, he and his brothers constructed a flat roofed, three-room log and adobe structure for their residence. They then purchased a handful of cattle for starters. Castle Rock was in a remote northwest region of the grant, nearly abutting the Sangre de Christo Mountains, thirty miles from grant headquarters in Cimarron, thus at the moment away from the company's scope of interest. A small community had already taken root, started and encouraged by Dan Griffin and his wife Jennie. From Alabama, the thirty-four-year-old Griffin was a lawyer and well-traveled, having voyaged to Hawaii, the Sandwich Islands and San Francisco, and lucratively employed in various enterprises. He now ran a successful mercantile store in Castle Rock and owned a large ranch. He was a popular citizen of the settlement, and like the rest of the community, anti-grant. They all looked hopefully forward to the bogus grant's nullification and freedom from the fear of eviction, and their own independent farming and stock-raising futures. But for some reason the settlers and the Manbys didn't hit it off. It may have been their aloofness and "Englishness" which put a wedge between them and their neighbors. If true, it more pointedly may have been Arthur and his arrogance, his haughty standoffishness failing to create an endearing air.

One hot afternoon, during a stretch of time when the local streams were running low and the spring runoff was exceptionally bleak, Griffin requested permission to water some of his stock at the Manby pond. Arthur refused. Whatever was going through Manby's mind, his denial was anathema to the rules of the range, and after this it was downhill for the English trio. Suspicion and gossip soon spread that the brothers may be agents for the grant, snoopers who were gathering information. Too, it was rumored Arthur was selling bogus quitclaim deeds, and Griffin had purchased some of the worthless paper from him.

About ten in the morning on 11 May 1884, Griffin paid Arthur a visit to discuss something. Some thought it may have been about some "deeds" Arthur had sold him. But more gravely serious it may have been over the earlier denial of Arthur not allowing him use of the Manby pond to water his animals, still a sore point between them. Jocelyn was in the kitchen preparing breakfast while Alfred was in the barn milking a cow. Before long a volatile argument erupted between the two men in the yard and a desperate struggle ensued. Jocelyn, hearing shots, peered out the window. He saw the smaller Arthur grappling with the beefy Griffin who held a pistol. Arthur had the man's gun-hand in the air as several more shots went off. Jocelyn temporarily abandoned his breakfast-making chores to grab a rifle and coolly lay it across the window sill. Taking a careful bead and waiting for a clean shot, he squeezed off a round. Alfred meanwhile, hearing the shooting, had run from the barn and upon his entry on the battlefield caught Jocelyn's slug as it tore through Griffin. The bullet hit Alfred on a front pants button, deflected enough to travel around his body on one side, then drop into his boot. He carried a long scar across his side the rest of his life.

Another slightly different version of the event had Jocelyn running into the yard with a pistol at the sight of the men struggling. Moments later Alfred appeared behind him in the doorway and saw Griffin on the ground with Arthur and Jocelyn bending over him. Emerging from Griffin's house next door burst Abe Howe and Garnet Lee, where Griffin spent the night. The two heard the shots over breakfast. It seems Howe, Lee, and Alfred emerged too late to witness what actually took place.

Arthur immediately rode to Raton and retained an attorney, John H. Johns. At a hearing the next morning before Judge J. H. Hunt, Arthur claimed he had ordered Griffin off his property following a fierce argument. Instead, Griffin pulled a .38 and pointed it at Manby's head. Arthur ducked and grasped his gun hand, and as the men struggled the gun went off, missing Manby. Jocelyn suddenly appeared and fired his own gun. Griffin, hearing Jocelyn's shot, hesitated, during which Arthur claimed he tore the .38 out of his hand and shot him in the chest. While Griffin stood stunned, Arthur said he shot him a second time in the left temple as Howe and Lee came rushing out of Griffin's house. He claimed self-defense, as well as the right to order him off his property. Judge Hunt dismissed the case, accepting Manby's plea of self-defense.

Meanwhile, early the following year of 1885, Arthur became connected with a militia group headed by James P. Masterson, and it was almost his undoing. Jim was the youngest brother of William "Bat" Masterson. The young man had served in various law positions in Dodge City, Kansas as policeman, deputy, and town marshal from June 1878, through April 1881. In 1881, after a change in administrations, Bat and Jim were let go, and they left town. When Bat turned up in Trinidad, Colorado in February 1882, Jim was already there as a policeman. In April Bat was appointed city marshal. In May, Wyatt Earp and his party of six, including Doc Holiday, arrived from Tombstone, Arizona following the shootout at the O.K. Corral.

Bat was greatly responsible in helping Doc avoid extradition back to Tombstone to face murder charges. In the 1883 elections, after Bat was trounced by Lou Kreegar for sheriff, 637 to 248, he moved on to Denver. Jim remained in Trinidad.

By 1885, the Maxwell Land Grant fight in Colfax County was fifteen years old and still going strong. And yet, although the weight of political power and legal influence was on the side of the pro-granters, especially via the Santa Fe Ring, the grant people were experiencing frustrating times. It was mainly in the form of stubbornness, for many squatters and settlers still refused to unsquat, angrily resisting eviction. Also, the "fighting parson," Oscar P. McMains, the leader of the anti-granters, was a scourge to the pro-granters and the Santa Fe Ring, and many of the settlers looked up to him as their champion.

In November 1884, in Raton, pro-grant Sheriff John Hixenbaugh was seriously wounded when he attempted to arrest gunman Dick Rogers, wanted for the killing of Charles Miller. He would experience a leg amputation in time. Temporarily incapacitated, someone was needed to replace him as undersheriff until he could return to duty. Over the years, since 1870, the Ring occasionally resorted to hiring a "rent-a-thug" to help spur the more lackadaisical squatters to get the lead out. Now once again they were in the market for needed assistance in the form of an aggressive ejector of tenants. It was not only because of the loss of their chief law enforcer, but the eviction notices served were being greatly ignored. Yet whom could they turn to?

The last man they hired was Robert Clay Allison back in June 1874, but he resigned his services in December 1875, much to the enraged chagrin of Governor and Ring advocate Samuel B. Axtell. This time pro-grant attorney Frank Springer of Colfax County was said to have turned to his friends of the Santa Fe Railroad for a potential recruit. The railroad then queried Wells, Fargo, who in turn tapped the shoulder of the noted Wyatt Earp. Enthusiastically,

Frank and his rancher brother Charles invited Earp to Cimarron, who turned up with his *amoretta*, Josephine Marcus. Yet all the wining and dining by the Springers was in vain, for Josie put her foot down as if to say, one Tombstone a lifetime was enough. Exit Earp. But on his way out Wyatt was said to have dropped the name of his old buddy Bat's brother, Jim, who just happened to be up in Trinidad. With bated breath Jim was quickly contacted, and to their sighs of relief he accepted.

On 23 January 1885, in Raton, James Masterson, thirty, was sworn into office by Sheriff Hixenbaugh. Jim, described as dour and misanthropic as well as deadly and a fast-draw, also seemed not to be hamstrung by neither tact nor diplomacy, for he bragged he was out to "get" Dick Rogers for shooting the sheriff. An added incentive may have been the $500 reward Governor Lionel Sheldon placed on Rogers' head. But to be fair he may have wanted people to know he took his job seriously, so didn't beat around the bush in announcing his professional intent. Either way, the boast would return to haunt him embarrassingly like a bad echo, and the reverberation occurred not a month after he took office and made the brag. While his accepting the invitation as undersheriff in the smoldering atmosphere of Colfax County may have been the most grievous error of his career, his second mistake undoubtedly occurred a week later on 3 February.

On that Friday evening he agreed to accompany seven or eight of his friends for a visit to Chihuahua, the red-light district on the northern fringe of Trinidad. As the last man to enter the door of Williams & Sargent's dance hall, he was immediately grabbed by several armed men of the Dick Rogers gang. Ed King grasped him by the right thumb and twisted him around while Tom Whealington shoved a gun in his back. Rogers approached his quarry heated and cursing; Masterson matched him verbally. Without another word Rogers drew his Colt and began pistol-whipping him on the head and face. Trying to deflect the blows with his arms, Masterson fell to the floor. He was then repeatedly kicked. Half-conscious, the lawman's gun belt with holstered weapon was unbuckled and taken as he was jerked to his feet. Shoved out on the dance floor, Rogers ordered him to dance a jig. As he groggily did so, Rogers told him to dance faster as he pumped shots into the floor at his feet. The gang guffawed at the sight of Masterson's erratic shuffle as he wiped oozing blood from his face and eyes. As he grew dizzy and weak, Rogers finally told him to sit at a table and keep his mouth shut. Gratefully dropping into a chair, he laid his battered head in his arms with a groan as the drunken revelers continued their partying for perhaps another half hour, then left.

Two weeks later the Governor raised the ante for Rogers to $1,000. Added to the $500 for the murder of Miller was $500 for the attempted killing of Hixenbaugh.

On 17 February, Masterson sent a brief note to Attorney General Edward Bartlett:

"My Dear Sir.

I send you today Muster Roll and other Papers. Will forward Bond tonight. We are well organized and ready for service. Please fill requisition at your earliest convenience. We need rations and few other supplies. Please instruct me how to obtain them.

Your Obedient Servant,
James Masterson, Co."

The next day the Governor gave the final approval for a territorial militia, designated as Company H, and Attorney General Bartlett sent Masterson the commissions and the necessary paperwork. Its officers were Captain, James Masterson; Second Lieutenant, deputy sheriff Jessie W. Lee; First Sergeant, John M. Cavanaugh. Its strength was reported at forty enlisted men. The following day two cases of arms arrived at the express office in Raton addressed to: "James Masterson, Captain, Company H, Territorial Militia." On Saturday, two days later, Captain Masterson and his men mounted up and began beating the bushes for Dick Rogers and his gang.

Masterson's militia were far from greeted warmly, for it was believed by the general populace they were just another strong-arm bunch brought in to help the Ring evict the squatters. Too, the Raton anti-militia men also protested. During the weekend while Masterson was scouring the countryside for Rogers, John C. Holmes, the editor of the *Weekly Independent*, made a quick trip to Santa Fe for a meeting with the Governor. He had with him a petition signed by eighty-eight citizens protesting the Masterson group, and which ended with the statement, "Masterson's militia will be the cause of more bloodshed."

The Governor was both surprised and puzzled at the citizen's petition, for not a week previous a "Mister Penhale" of Raton insisted strongly for an appointed force in Colfax County to maintain law and order. He described Dick Rogers and his gang as a group of wild renegades running the town as they wished, and that people were leaving in fear of their lives. Holmes answered he had no idea who Mister Penhale was, but the man lied. Attorney General Bartlett then asked Holmes about the Maxwell Grant Company's difficulty of enforcing court decrees against the settlers. The editor retorted that the hiring of gunmen like Masterson was not a sensible solution. Yet the Attorney General continued eulogizing the militia and their law-enforcing properties, and of how Raton should be proud of Masterson's company and not oppose it. Holmes saw he was getting nowhere, so asked before leaving if he could have a list of the members of the company. Bartlett gladly complied. With list in hand he returned to Raton. What the incisive, or intuitive, editor found was not too surprising to him. Holmes and several close friends checked out the roster and found that of the forty so-called enlisted men, close to thirty were paper members. Many names were inscribed without knowledge or permission of certain citizens. Besides being a fraudulent organization, a dozen men were drawing the pay of forty, leaving them open to charges of forgery and perjury. The irate paper members voluntarily signed affidavits of protest which Holmes and Charles M. Bayne swiftly presented to the Governor.

Sheldon was furious at being so duped and ordered the militia's immediate disbandment, aborting its seven-day lifespan. He sent United States Marshal John A. Williams to find and notify them of his order, and to prepare themselves for legal consequences. When located and informed of their termination, the marshal sped off a note to the Attorney General on 3 March:

> "Dear Sir(.)
> Enclosed pleas(e) find returns (?) every thing is all right and the Militia have returned to Raton(.) please see to my Fees and oblige(.)
> respectfully, John A. Williams, Deputy U.S. Marshal."

But alas, contrary to the marshal's assessment, everything was not all right, for Masterson and his followers blew up. Returning to Raton, they proceeded causing a small riot, riding up and down the street shouting, cursing and terrifying citizens, while shooting out a few windows here and there. Masterson spotted businessman H.E. Herndon on the sidewalk, one of the paper members, and walked up to him, upbraiding him with a drawn six-gun, vowing he would kill every man who signed the complaint of being on his roster. Moments later he met merchant D.W. Stevens on the street and smacked him with his Colt, laying him out on the ground.

Young George Curry, twenty-four, saw it all, and after helping his employer to his feet, without hesitation began summoning every able-bodied man he could find. At eleven that night, at a hastily put-together town meeting at the local skating rink, 200 angry citizens gathered. Curry organized the group into a vigilante force, and all saloons and stores were immediately locked down. They began patrolling the streets with one thing in mind: the capture and confinement of Masterson and every one of his cohorts, which they were successful in doing before the night was out. Hardly two days earlier, Dick Rogers had given himself up. At a hearing he was charged with three counts: the killing of Miller, the wounding of Hixenbaugh, and the assault on Masterson. Pleading self-defense to the Miller killing, he was released on a $1,000 bond. In a twist of irony, he was elected as head of the vigilance committee, and to Masterson's mortification, eagerly assisted in the rounding up of his former antagonists.

Yet it appears a few of the ex-militia avoided capture, including Arthur Manby. But Arthur was quite indignant at being labeled one of Masterson's men, and penned a letter to the *Raton Comet* expressing his resentment. He explained he had absolutely nothing to do with Masterson or his company; that he and his brothers were carried as members without their knowledge. He claimed to have been in Santa Fe during the Raton riot seeking an attorney to represent him in his upcoming Griffin murder trial. Trouble was, several Raton citizens were positive they saw Arthur among the riders with Masterson, including George Curry.

At nine the following morning the skating rink was the meeting place of 600 Ratonites and their prisoners. It was decided that Masterson and all non-residents of the defunct militia must leave town at once, and to never return. Bona fide resident deputy sheriff Jesse Lee, Arthur Manby, John Cavanaugh and one other were allowed to return to their homes. An escort committee was appointed to deliver the rest to the Colorado line, seven miles north.

Captain of the mounted escorts was none other than Dick Rogers. After the assembly's adjournment, the prisoners were taken to a restaurant, given a farewell meal, then marched afoot up Wootton Pass. What words were exchanged between Rogers and Masterson and his ghost militia can only be imagined, but whatever insults were heaped upon them, they were more than fortunate at the rare civilized demonstration of rope-less justice.

Perhaps Arthur Manby thought that by associating himself with the Masterson coterie he would endear himself to the Maxwell Land Grant Company. Too, it may have been because he was nervous over the possibility of eviction, and the calculated risk was worth the try, for the grant people held all the cards anyway. He certainly wished like any homesteader to hold and develop his ranch for years to come; to grow crops, raise cattle, sheep or horses. But the manner in which he sought economic security was no more solid than quicksand. By calculatingly hooking his hopes to men hired to dash the hopes of other dreamers on the other side of the fence was merely a shifting of the nightmare. All he did was help aggravate the situation as did Jim Masterson with his collection of imported gunmen. But Masterson had no illusions as to who he was: a hired man. Manby was the wily intriguer on Jim's back.

But did he really ride with them? He may have, but at times it is a bit difficult to believe he did, for his pattern of behavior show him to be a designing, crafty man. He always seemed to operate from within, or behind himself. An agent of secrecy, coverture was his way. But galloping amid a pack of howling cowboys on a street in Raton wasn't exactly insurance for invisibility. Perhaps he miscalculated. Or maybe it was a one-shot event to him, to show the militia he was with them, and Captain Masterson would spread the endorsement to his grant hirelings, "That ol' Manby is OK!" Just one ride he may have thought, for the sake of property security. Then stay on his ranch long as he could, too busy to join them on their future raids. But the quasi-militia died a quick death once exposed for what they were, and with them and their captain run out of town. Arthur may have done some heavy sweating himself, picturing hoofing those miles to the border under the whipping curses of Dick Rogers. It would have been worse than an eviction, for he could never return.

Six months later the shooting of Dan Griffin finally caught up with the Manbys. Griffin's wife Jennie was left understandably enraged at the shoulder-shrugging dismissal of Arthur by Judge Hunt. Consequently she protested vigorously and strenuously with family and friends throughout the summer, seeking her husband's day in court. Eventually successful, on 29 September 1885, Arthur and Jocelyn were indicted for the shooting and bonded out at $10,000 each. Arthur made a trip to Santa Fe and wisely retained Tom Catron as defending attorney, one of the chief magicians of the Santa Fe Ring. Things dragged on for another year before a grand jury was finally formed in September 1886 to examine the evidence. E.L. Hubbard was foreman.

The jury accepted the finding of two bullets fired into Griffin's body, except for dire contradictions. One was in his left side below the ribs but *not* in the chest, while the second was squarely in his forehead, *not* in his left temple. Each wound "had the breadth of one inch and the depth of six inches." A true bill for murder was found against the two for "unlawfully, willfully, feloniously, maliciously, of their aforethought and from a premeditated design to effect the death of him the said Daniel B. Griffin." Melvin W. Mills, District Attorney for Colfax, Taos and Rio Arriba Counties, and staunch Santa Fe Ring adherent, was prosecutor. The Manby brothers were ordered to trial.

After nineteen challenges and dismissals, the final selected jurors were: Isadore Baca, Edward C. Clothier, also foreman, Carlos Comay, Anastacio Fernandez, Ramon Garcia, Juan Guam(?), Mathias Heck, M.A. McMartin, Pablo Montoya, Andres Ramariz,

Juan Sanduval and William Shaffer. Jack Mitchell was the alternative juror.

The outcome was swift and predictable, for Tom Catron, the rotund conjuror of Santa Fe performed adroitly. At the conclusion of the legal ceremonies on 18 September, the foreman read, "We the jury find the defendants Arthur Manby and Jocelyn Manby not guilty." One rumor claimed the influencing alchemic factor was a $1,000 "fee" from each of the three brothers.

Arthur, understandably, after the dual fortunes of escaping disagreeable consequences from his short "enlistment" in Masterson's Militia, and his and Jocelyn's lightening-swift verdict of innocence in the Griffin murder trial, may have experienced a brief flash of invulnerability. But it undoubtedly carried the aroma of cynicism in realizing their freedom had a price, that without the juice of payola in the Griffin case, he and Jocelyn may have had to serve some time. It increased Arthur's bitterness toward the Ring, feeling as an outsider because of his inability to insert himself somehow into their good graces. To add to his annoyance, he and Jocelyn were soon dunned for delinquent back taxes to the sum of $191.60. The following year they were hit for another $400, which Arthur was successful in contesting and bringing down to $378.75.

About this time Jocelyn decided on a short vacation to England with his friend, Norman Raynor. On their return trip in May 1887, approaching New York through a thick fog one day out, their ship, the *Celtic*, rammed the outgoing *Britannic*. The bow of the *Celtic* struck the *Britannic* twice, driving herself into its side. Confusion, din, and the moans of the injured caused a near panic aboard the *Britannic*, for the casualties of several passengers killed included one child decapitated. Among its voyagers were the Roosevelts, Elliot and his daughter, two and one half year-old Eleanor. They were with those transferred by lifeboat to the *Celtic*, and Manby and Raynor graciously volunteered their stateroom to the Roosevelts. A few months following their return to New Mexico, Jocelyn took out citizenship papers and married Louella Young.

Perhaps with a touch of spite, or peevishness, Arthur began grazing cattle on Maxwell Company pasture. In January 1889, the company filed suit against the Manbys and Raynor, and in June filed an injunction against them. It is possible Arthur knew all along what he was doing, for he smugly reminded the grant people that their title was still being contested in the courts and was as yet undecided, giving them weak grounds in their suit. In November the company was forced to drop the injunction. But controlling masters are unforgiving masters and dislike having the error of their ways pointed out to them, especially by minor, irascible footmen. In consequence, the Manbys were delivered a summons which resulted in their eviction from grant property. Arthur's victory turning Cadmean further enraged him.

In October 1891, Jocelyn moved the last of his cattle off the land. Being a natural stockman who loved his work he stayed with it as long as he could, being for a time a livestock dealer, particularly sheep. After the loss of their ranch he worked for a time for the JJ outfit, owned by the Prairie Land & Cattle Company. He next relocated to Trinidad, Colorado, then finally Denver where he settled with his family in nearby Edgewater, shifting to the profession of real estate.

Arthur and Alfred, still bachelors, moved to the VT Bar Ranch east of Raton where they worked for a time. In the early 1900s, Alfred returned to England to marry Rita Robinson. He then brought his bride to New Mexico. The couple lived on the Sugarite north of Raton, then moved later to the old 47 Ranch on the Mora River near Shoemaker. They then resided for a time at the Joe Watrous ranch in Watrous, until finally moving off to Canada.

Arthur, forced to abandon his ranching ambitions turned to mining. He dallied for a time in the Moreno Valley region of the grant, ireful and still smarting from the humiliation of ouster. While he picked up a few mining properties he thought had potential, in the back of his mind he still clung to the obstinate obsession of owning a vast estate, envying and despising the grant people for both, the extensive acreage they held in their hands, and the small amount of pasture which they deprived him. The love-hate romance gnawed at him like searing acid, festering his resentment night and day, while feeding his inner fever for success.

Exactly when Arthur moved off to Taos is uncertain, but he related a lurid tale of how one night he supposedly shot a man to death prior to his leaving the area in the 1890s. Spending the night at the St. James Hotel in Cimarron, he claimed he was awakened in the early hours by someone pacing just outside his room. The party knocked, then attempted entry by turning the door knob. Finding it locked, he slowly walked away. Arthur, suspecting an assassin, quietly got out of bed, took his revolver in hand, then went to the door. Opening it cautiously he spied a man stealthily walking away. Without hesitation he pumped several bullets into the man's back then packed and fled.

Another of his spun yarns? Probably so, since the law would know whom to look for after checking with the clerk and hotel register. He would have had little chance of escaping far, for his destination was only across the mountains to Taos, hardly sixty miles away. Perhaps the imaginative fib was a hostile transference of sorts to settle his steaming, unsettled mind, an extension of his protesting rage against his heartless ouster from the grant.

Having to leave his ranch was no small thing for him, and forever after the very mention of the Maxwell Grant left a bad taste in his mouth, while the Santa Fe Ring made him want to retch. Although left awry and frustrated in his plans to gain a financial and propertied foothold in this frontier corner of America, he refused to admit or accept defeat. Rather, it fed him as raw meat thrown to a ravenous beast. He would show them. There are more ways than one to skin a cat. The time he spent working his claims in the Moreno Valley south of Elizabethtown helped cool his fevered brain and readjust his focus. The gold strike on Mount Baldy was still going strong, as were a handful of claims scattered along the valley. But most were small or soon played out. After a few months of having no luck on his own digs, he tossed in his shovel and sluice box for a move to Taos. With blood-lust in his heart and that old endless vision of personal wealth in his imagination, this poseur, sham and confidence man pressed on. Yes. He would weave out his fate on the loom of his ambitions to attain his dream. It was there, he could taste it. Just around the corner.

Part 2

Clotho

The Taos Cresset of 1899 and 1990 was filled with items concerning Manby and his persistent prospecting for gold and silver throughout the vicinity. He is referred to several times as "Colonel" Manby, and the stories reflect a strong flavor of success and prosperity, a man on the way up. There was also the mention of a journey to Mexico.

Since arriving in Taos some years previous, Arthur had been quite busy, driven in fact. He vowed personally to leave no stone unturned in his quest for riches and renown, in that order. And as his luck would have it, before too long chance loaned a hand.

One morning as he was strolling along Taos plaza, he passed a small knot of men before the courthouse in animated conversation. Manby picked up on the Spanish and paused, soon becoming a member of the yammering group. The topic was a Taos land grant.

"Which one?" he asked in Spanish, suddenly agog.

"The Martinez," someone replied.

He had never heard of it but a legal session concerning it would soon take place at the courthouse in Santa Fe. On the verge of trembling he got the details, then hastily left the men for his hotel room to pack for his journey to the state capitol, seventy miles south. All along his ride he was feverishly excited, knowing this was his time, his moment. A land grant! Echoes of the Maxwell reverberated through his memory and imagination. Yes, this was his moment in history! He was a great believer in fate, but also that one must keep open to any opportunity which showed itself, then have the courage to immediately act upon it. To give fate a hand, a push. And he knew deep in his soul this was his time to push, to give the old girl all the help she needed!

Arriving in Santa Fe the next morning, he grabbed a room at the Exchange Hotel on the crowded plaza. Bathing, he fell into bed for a good, solid sleep, which was impossible during the stage ride. Waking, he dressed in a clean change of clothes brought with him, arranged to have his discarded clothing laundered, ate lunch in the restaurant, then strolled about the town. He had been here several times before back in 1886, conferring with Tom Catron, his attorney in the Griffin killing. Meandering aimlessly a few days he wryly saw things hadn't changed much from its mud-brick appearance and summer dustiness. Trying to relax and play tourist was difficult for him, for his thoughts were on the hearing and he was impatient to know what was going to take place, what legal and historical ramifications he had to comprehend in order to make his move, or moves, on the grant. No use thinking on it or worrying it to death now, he continued reminding himself, not until he could get the full story anyway. But his brain was like a tinder box on a freight train, or a giant magnet drawing energy from all around him; he was unable to rest a moment. His grant!

On the morning of the session he made his way to the courthouse and entered the room where the hearing was to be held. The room was large, well-lit by tall, wide windows, curtained by stained, brown canvas drapes, and furnished with rows of tired looking benches. Several overly-used desks and chairs were up front, peopled by whom Manby took to be legal personages, lawyers and judges dressed in rumpled cheap suits with wrinkled white shirts and ties. He saw a handful of people already seated on the benches as he claimed a center aisle seat near the front. While he sat with pad and pencil in hand, a few others trickled in.

Looking about he could not help but notice that everything was brown, and in his bias was unable to appreciate the low-toned frowziness of everything when compared to civilized, immaculate England. The walls, ceiling, floor, benches, people, all brown as the mud bricks they used in all their structures they call adobe. Much as he tried to remain neutral in his new environment, he was naturally wired against the ignorant masses, and could not help but hold up England as the cultural apex of the universe, found it impossible to not snobbily look down upon the frontier west as a collection of humble hamlets filled with unwashed and uneducated country bumpkins. Santa Fe was like an enlarged Taos, and much of New Mexico that he had seen. Everything brown, beige and tan. The color of earth. All that sand with dust clouds everywhere, from horses, carts, wagons, trying to keep from choking at times with a handkerchief over the mouth, especially on windy days. It can be so maddening. In England he never knew so much dust and sand existed in the world and in one place. Yet now here he was, filled with distaste with everything around him, and preparing to fight tooth and nail for a piece of that dusty ground called the Martinez Grant.

Briefly described, in 1716, Antonio Martinez, a New Mexican, petitioned Captain Felix Martinez, Governor and Captain-General of New Mexico in Santa Fe, for a grant of land in the valley of Taos. It formerly belonged to Sergeant-Major Lucero de Godoi. The Captain granted the petition with the provision that the Indians of the Pueblo of Taos be notified in case of any objections. Since they had none, three days later an assembly made up of Captain Martinez and his officials, the Cacique and other elders of the Pueblo, and Antonio Martinez, proceeded to the tract of land and went through the ritual of boundary description and possession.

In 1821, Mexico, after winning independence from Spain following 300 years of crushing, intolerant dominance, confirmed all Spanish land grants in its northern province of New Mexico. Then in 1844, after the War of Mexico with the United States, it lost its northern territories of Texas, New Mexico, Arizona and California to the United States. At the Treaty of Guadalupe four years later, the United States recognized all land grants of New Mexico. But over the years the legal process of recognizing the validity of grants was painstakingly slow, so in 1891, a United States Court of Private Land Claims was established hoping to expedite the procedure.

It was now 1892, and the hearing Manby was listening to was whether to confirm or deny the Martinez/de Godoi Grant.

The four claimants from Taos, three Martinez's, and a Garcia, were sworn in before the five judges. Asked for proof of being descendants and rightful heirs of Antonio Martinez, the men had no documents to speak of, pleading memory and knowledge of lineage. But the court held no sympathy for verbal claims or demands. It was adamant. It needed solid proof. Too, it lay for so long forgotten there was no definite idea as to the acreage claimed, nor where the borders actually lay. Those questions had to be answered satisfactorily before the court authorities would even think of answering to its validity. After a period of unsatisfactory wrangling and arid debate, the court adjourned.

With Manby's imagination swirling and salivating, upon his return to Taos he decided to make a horseback journey throughout a portion of the roughly one hundred square miles of the vaguely bordered grant. Loading his saddlebags with edibles and necessities, slipping a rifle into his scabbard and a .38 in his holster, and accompanied by his German Shepherd, he forked his black horse Nigger, and was gone for the better part of two weeks. The miles and days he spent in the rough inspection of what he now embraced as "his" property further fortified his obsession for its ownership, and that it was his destiny to do so. He felt as a conquistador come to reclaim what was once his, and would not be denied.

Over 61,000 acres, it was shaped roughly as a lop-sided, somewhat fir-thatched triangle. Its western edge ran for about ten miles along the eastern bank of the Rio Grande, while its elongated deltoidal borders pulled away from the river. The steep, rugged gorge gave him a breathtaking view a thousand feet above the Rio. Gazing down, between him and the flowing water an occasional hawk soared and glided from cliff to cliff seeking prey, sometimes suspending itself on currents of wind, scanning the rocks for movement. He remembered as a child in Morcambe being mesmerized by them as he admired their graceful, fluid maneuvers high in the sky, hauntingly frozen in space with their wide wings spread, watching and waiting. Now and then he would see one suddenly dive like a rocket for an unsuspecting rodent or rabbit, snaring it in its talons at the bottom of its swooping loop, then soar off to a safe niche to feed. He immediately felt a strong affinity with them, an identity, a bond. Hawks! As he now studied a pair between the mile-apart canyon walls, slowly curling in wide circles toward the river below, he felt they were an omen, a portent, a sign. They are guarding my grant. Mine! The more he peered across and up and down the river a mile below him as he rode along its shear precipice, the more he felt at home. This triangular wedge of turf was his, his motherland. Over one hundred square miles. His daydreaming took him across the Atlantic back to England: Eardley. Yes, he must have a conference with Eardley!

Once back in Taos he hurriedly prepared for a trip to Morcambe. He grabbed a stage for Pueblo, Colorado, a train for New York, and a ship to England, and all along the way his visions were paved with gold. He'd show the Maxwell Grant swine and the damned Santa Fe Ring! The Martinez Grant, soon to be re-christened the Manby Grant, filled his brain all during the journey. It wasn't as big as the Maxwell, but it would do nicely. The Arthur Rochford Manby Grant. Oh, what a sweet and heavenly ring it had! Its very name as he whispered it clasped him in ecstatic fervor. When alone and out of shot of an audience he would practice aloud with theatrical robustness, and as he did so the syllables would roll and reverberate in his skull as a great bell tolling in celebration. "The Arthur Rochford Manby Grant!"

Just before Arthur's trip to Morcambe, a survey had been completed on 14 February 1895, and it came out to 61,604.48 acres. To make his move at purchasing what he could from the various eighty heirs when it was finally approved he would need money, and lots of it. The backing of financiers is what he aimed for, and with Eardley's business connections it was he who was the fulcrum of his purchase. On his way to England Arthur stopped in New York to discuss his elaborate plans with financial brokers whose strong interest left him further encouraged. Assuring them, he looked forward to near-future documentation and plats of the grant, and that he would certainly keep them in mind. Then he left for England.

Arthur's unbridled enthusiasm so overwhelmed Eardley that he took him to London for introductions to business cohorts. Arthur once again created his magic, painting a colorful description of the grant and all its economic potentialities, from the scattered gold mines to an army of settlers forming farming communities across its one hundred square miles, to the gradual and undeniable influx of a wide range of businesses which in turn would sprout towns, and even a railroad. And he did not fail to mention his plans for the Rio Grande hot springs spa.

"There simply would be no end to its economic growth!" he re-emphasized again and again with the sparkling eyes of a true believer, who held in his desperate hands his ambitious future.

Manby did his work well, for Eardley and his eager investor-friends exuberantly exclaimed, "Arthur, purchase the grant and we will be only too happy to invest in its development!"

"Gentlemen," Arthur's voice intoned hoarsely, wiping his brow and face with his handkerchief following his heated presentation. "It is as good as purchased. Believe me!" Unable to contain himself, being a helpless ham to hyperbole, he howled in theatrical emphasis, "We are on the threshold of owning the wealthiest section of America today!" With that he emptied his goblet of Chateaunauf-du-Pape and dramatically flung the empty glass into the blazing fireplace where it exploded.

"Bravo!" saluted the company with echoing unleashed elation in a rain of goblets.

Before sailing from England he borrowed a goodly amount from Eardley as "starter seed" for their enterprise. "For our grant," Arthur emphasized with an oleaginous smile to ease any doubt which his older sibling may have been harboring. Eardley beamed, still mesmerized by his brother's dramatic performance over the London dinner. Arthur over the years would proudly look back upon that night as his finest moment.

With him on his departure he also took some of his mother's paintings, scenes done while he was a child at her side daubing his eager heart out to please her, scenes he would look upon poignantly the rest of his life, profoundly experiencing exactly those summer hours of her presence, and of a sweet lost kingdom. Before leaving Morcambe he spent a moist-eyed hour at her grave, speaking to her, thanking her for her love and devotion, and her belief in him.

Upon his return to Taos, Manby checked the progress on the Martinez Grant and found it had yet to be approved and patented. So he waited with patient anticipation, turning to mining. He visited the latest gold strike in tiny Amizette, hardly fifteen miles northeast of Taos. The hamlet was named after the wife of the prospector who struck the find, Al Helphinstine. Manby wasted no time and rode out on horseback to look things over. The small encampment swelled to a population of around 300, but the gold was of poor quality and not worth the expense of trekking it down the canyon. In a year or two the community was abandoned. A year or so later a new find up the same canyon was made by William Frazer. Frazer contacted a New Jersey banker named Albert C. Twining to invest, and the financier did so enthusiastically. The new town was called Twining, and a $300,000 smelter was built to help eliminate the cost of transporting the ore. But sadly the molten ore adhered itself to the sides of the oven like paste, and the business went bankrupt. Before too long banker Twining was shipped off to prison for embezzlement, and Frazer had to find a new partner. He found one in Jack Bidwell. But it wasn't too long before their partnership also suffered a snag, when Bidwell discovered that Frazer was stealing. With no compunction whatsoever, Bidwell hunted him down and shot him to death. The operations then halted, some of the cabins were moved off to Taos, and the mill was accidently burned to the ground in 1932.

The echoes of the tragedy in the Twining misadventure failed to dissuade Manby from his own pursuit of El Dorado, or whatever it took to attain his dream, whether in mining for gold or grasping for his real estate empire. Or both, if he had his way. But there were bad apples in every profession, that was a given. It was a professional hazard. One just had to be careful when choosing a partner, and be doubly cautious after that. Hell, one bad apple won't spoil the tree. Just tear off the branch and continue pruning.

It was at Amizette where Manby rode out to spend a few days checking its potential that he met the old sourdough, Columbus Ferguson.

Columbus "Jack" Ferguson, sometimes referred to as "Lum," was born in Galena, Illinois, on 12 January 1847. He was the second of twelve children in a brood of eight males and four females. The first born, Franklin, was killed in the Civil War fighting with forces under Union General Sterling Price. During Price's hapless two-month raid into Missouri, Franklin Ferguson fell at Brush Creek on 23 October 1874, just four days after his nineteenth birthday. Columbus may have served for a time with the Ninth Kansas Cavalry. Their father Elijah was from Kentucky, their mother Marianne "Molly" Quinche, from Minnesota. It appears the two met in Illinois where they married on 29 January 1845.

Exactly when Columbus made the move to New Mexico is speculative, but over the years he would become quite familiar with mines in the Taos region. It has been mentioned he had been drawn to several of its digs, such as Gold Hill. Too, in the intervening years he met and married Juanita Medina, a Taosina, in June 1883. He was thirty-six and she thirty-three. They had three children; Luis born in June 1884, Francesca in November 1886, and Terecita on 11 August 1888.

In the mid-1860s, he was one of thousands of miners who made their way to the rich gold fields of the Baldy Mountain region, about sixty miles northeast of Taos. The big strike was the Aztec Mine to the east of Baldy, and the community of Elizabethtown to the west of it quickly burst to nearly 7,000. Here he met a Pennsylvanian German named William Stone with whom he claimed to have partnered. They developed a pair of claims: the Mystic, just below the western brow of Baldy and about one and one half miles from the Aztec, and the Ajax, two miles southwest of the Mystic.

On one of his breaks from his Baldy claims, he moved with his wife and three children to the new discovery at Amizette. Renting a small adobe shed he set about hunting for the yellow stuff. At a mining camp communication was usually centered around the latest news of finds, and the quality and quantity of the ore, and before long he realized as others did that it was of poor quality.

One afternoon Ferguson was afoot inspecting a rocky hillside when from around a knoll a few yards away a mounted stranger suddenly loomed before him. The horseman startlingly reined up. Ferguson's defensive radar went off, being in a profession whose natural enemies were robbers, thieves and claim-jumpers. He automatically sidled toward his rifle which rested against a tree-stump nearby. Manby leaned forward casually with both palms purposely on his saddle horn in a purposeful show of empty hands, greeting him with a, "Good afternoon, sir."

"Good afternoon."

"Any luck?"

"Nope. I think the place is highly over-rated."

"Me too. Nothing to write home about."

"That's for sure."

Manby sensed suspicion from the miner and did not blame him, being of the same turn of mind. Slowly and carefully dismounting his black mount he walked a few steps toward him, reins in hand. "I have some mining properties west of here in the Moreno Valley in Colfax County. Picked them up when I quit my ranch up on the Maxwell Grant. Live in Taos now."

"That right?" eyed Ferguson in an effort to measure who the stranger might be. Clothes worn but expensive, like his western hat, a beaver. Boots scuffed, muddy, but of good quality. No badge, but a holstered gun on his hip to match Ferguson's and everyone else's in the region. Winchester butt-forward in a sleeve on his horse. Saddle, reins, and trappings of fine work, and horse a stout breed. A monied man of breeding.

Arthur extended his hand. "Manby's the name. Arthur Rochford Manby."

"Ferguson," he answered, extending his own. "Columbus Ferguson."

"Greetings, dear sir," grinned Manby somewhat tightly, not used to smiling on strangers.

"Sounds like you're an easterner. Or maybe an English?"

"From England, sir," came his proud tone. "To be sure."

"Well, I'm from Illonoi myself. Been in these parts many a year now, digging and panning about. How long you be from England?"

"Came over in eighty-three. Had an inheritance I wished to do something with. Ranched for a while up in Castle Rock. Sold out and moved to Taos where I went into real estate."

"Ahhh, you be the fella sniffing around the Martinez Grant?"

Surprised, Manby answered tautly, "The same, Mister Ferguson. The very same."

"Don't be shocked, sir," he grinned. "News travels fast in these parts. Good and bad both. And call me Columbus."

"And I'd be pleased if you would address me as Arthur."

Their exchanges came more easily and natural as they went on discussing various topics the next hour and half, and they clicked, finding a warm camaraderie despite their social, cultural and economic disparity. The half-truths they wove between their tales smoothly blended and dove-tailed with whatever opinions each held of the other, accepting the fact that every man lied; some out of necessity, others for entertainment or ego-need, and still others just for the desire to give a story a good twist. It was an indigenous trait of the male ego, and harmless as long as it caused no dire difficulty. Columbus also revealed his claims around Baldy, the richest area in New Mexico at the moment. Manby was quite impressed, adding modestly that his own claims there had yet to show anything.

"Arthur, unless you're in a hurry, please have dinner with us. Do you like lamb?"

"Yes, indeed."

"Then you will enjoy the lamb chili of my wife. Most delicious, let me tell you!"

"I would be a fool to deny both, your hospitality and my stomach of such an opportunity! Lead on, Columbus!"

At a small adobe jacal not a mile later they reined up and tied their horses. Both unsheathed their rifles and entered the structure. As they stepped into the warmth of the humble abode, Ferguson's wife welcomed her husband warmly in Spanish, and he returned in kind.

"This is my wife, Juanita. She speaks some English but is

more comfortable in Spanish, which I've learned pretty well over the years."

Arthur, removing his hat and holding it before him over his chest, intoned a litany in perfect Spanish of his warm appreciation for her kindness and hospitality which left the woman awed and smiling. Columbus too was both surprised and pleased.

"And these are my children, Luis, Francesca, and Terecita. Say hello, young 'uns."

Luis, seven, and Francesca, five, stretched out a hand with a shy smile, emitting a barely perceptive "Hello." Three-year-old Terecita stood staring at the stranger in stoic assessment.

As their guest that night, Arthur spread his blanket and slept on the floor. The next morning after breakfast they discussed mining again avidly, both affirming to keep in touch.

"It's been a real pleasure meeting you, Arthur."

"And you too, Columbus. But let us not be strangers. With your knowledge and my financial backing perhaps we can do each other some good. What say?"

"You're a man after my heart, sir."

"Good. Then cast about and have some good news next time we meet."

"That I will, Arthur, that I will!"

Not too long after Manby returned home, he found to his great relief and delight a United States Patent had been granted for the Antonio Martinez/Lucero de Godoi Grant on 8 May 1896. With great glee and exuberance he quickly acquired a copy of the plat, studying it with the same intensity as a general about to launch a campaign. All this land is mine! he vowed, sliding his hands voraciously over the papered surface, caressing the triangular body of his vast domain. Every inch!

For the next two years he trolled about the grant and quietly bought up what properties he could from among the sixty-some heirs who would sell. He used an address in Elizabethtown in an effort to cloud his purpose. As usual, economic survival for the poor was always a struggle, in good times and bad, and it worked conveniently in favor of Manby's envisioned future fiefdom. The ones having a difficult time paying yearly taxes, let alone grubbing day after day in order to put food on the table were the easiest, some of them widows or elderly couples struggling in near-poverty. The cash Manby offered, which in better circumstances would have been laughed at, was too tempting to resist. But this gringo patron with his mixed air of strutting cockiness and holiday benevolence with fistfuls of cash was too irresistible, and a handful capitulated beneath his persistent pressuring and their wish for an escape from daily destitution.

By May 1898, seventeen pieces of real estate were his, seven of them huge chunks. He was also wise enough to acquire timber, grazing and mineral rights, with the right to build ditches, dams and reservoirs in order to later allow him to freely divert water from the Lucero and Seco Rivers for his future farmlands. On the northwestern edge of Taos, he combined a cluster of his purchased acreage, giving him a six-mile piece of home turf. He gathered a crew and began constructing his walled-in hacienda of nineteen rooms on the edge of the town's limits, building on to the small adobe structure already there. Clearing his grounds he prepared a section for molding his own adobe bricks, built stables for his future stock, laid out a large flower garden, and with the help of Taos Puebloan Tony Lujan, planted a row of trees along Pueblo Road. He moved as if driven by inner furies, and he probably was. Time was running short and he had so much to do. As a demanding taskmaster he drove his men, but paid well. During all this frenzied construction he wrote Eardley, describing the acreage he had picked up, colorfully painting all he had done and all he planned to do. Eardley, while impressed, but more practical, desired to see what his investment was looking like, so decided on a visit. Arthur, amenable, looked forward to his appearance, and told him he would meet him in Raton.

   While in Taos Eardley surreptitiously observed Arthur's daily comportment and was disturbed by his erratic behavior. He recalled the accident Arthur had in Morcambe when he fell off the second-story balcony at twenty and suffered a head injury. He was never quite the same. All treated his strangeness with a touch of light humor, believing that in time he would return to normal and all would be well. But instead he became thinner tempered, defensive, sometimes sinking into dark moods of suspicion and anger. Within a few years he began to be looked upon as the black sheep, so distanced from the family he had become. While theirs was not exactly what one could call a warm family hearth, it was also not unreasonably strict, but a certain amount of discipline and order was demanded for what their father thought was necessary for family unity and solidarity. Arthur now was beyond that, quarrelsome and borderline unmanageable. Only his mother could soften his harshness and growing granite attitude toward everyone and everything around him. She would often take him into the countryside to join her in painting, and of course he now as an adult had his own equipment of canvas, brushes and paints. It was the only time when he was soft, kind, and happy, when his demons left him in peace. After their mother had been laid to rest he became more trying than ever. When he decided to leave for America and the Maxwell Grant pastures, his siblings were glad to see him go. At his mother's grave he vowed to make her proud of him. He promised to do great things. Giving him travel fare and some pocket money, his homebound brothers and sisters in great relief cheerfully bon voyaged him, honestly hoping never to see him again.

   And now here was Eardley, caught up in his brother's schemes of endless wealth. It sounded all so solid and sane, so possible. Yet now he wondered to himself if he were not being duped, drawn into something beyond his comprehension, like into some dark country of which he had no guide or map. Looking into Arthur's shining eyes as he preached the sermon of economic nirvana, Eardley could not help but believe him. But a nervous apprehension gripped him which he could not explain. He found himself worrying and thinking defensively, as if he were in the company of a stranger, especially when several times his younger brother's temper erupted seizure-like over a trivial thing or two. Arthur's mind also meandered at times, going off reciting odd stories. He boasted of his connection with Jim Masterson and his militia company in Raton years previous, the brother of the famous Bat, who in turn was a crony of the even more famous Wyatt Earp. In Arthur's hyperbolic account he had all three gunmen gaining in their reputations through Arthur's reflected association with Jim Masterson. He spoke also of killing an upstart in his own backyard named Dan Griffin, shrugging it all off as a necessary action in the feral atmosphere of the wild west, and the necessity of occasionally having to take the law into one's own hands.

So Eardley now wondered to what degree his brother had been altered in his conduct due to his tumbling accident, whether the clay of circumstance had somehow cruelly re-sculpted his temperament. He was so normal much of the time, but when a certain excitement gripped him a fury would descend upon him which modified him drastically. As if he were in the company of another being, a monster inhabiting Arthur's body, a splitting away somehow. So odd, he mused.

Yet Eardley liked what he saw of his propertied accumulation after going through his paperwork with him one night. And he was impressed with Arthur's nineteen-room mansion, protectively and tastefully enwrapped by a thick adobe wall; the huge flower garden, the tree-lined Pueblo Road, the stables, the pastoral ambience of a handful of cows contentedly mooing and munching away. Arthur gleefully took them on a three-day horseback tour of the grant, "our grant," he emphasized with the sweep of his arm above the deep Rio

Grande gorge with the confident chortle of a victorious conquistador. Eardley was amazed and moved by the change in his persona the entire trip. Arthur was pleasant, confident and introspective; his brashness and hard-edged mein gone, replaced by an easy-going landlord effortlessly touring his extensive realm. Benevolent. Positive. Speaking soberly and seriously of the future towns, farms and railroad which would soon dot the landscape.

"A beautiful country," Arthur wistfully underscored. "My Mother Earth."

Eardley was completely seduced by Arthur's grand scheme, realizing he was onto something big. Yes, the dream was on the verge of becoming a reality. It was true. Eardley could see it. Yet he was still pragmatic enough to be cautious about leaping into the abyss. His sixth-sense was like a silent, protective alarm deep in his brain warning him away from the lip of the pit. His stay with Arthur those three months were otherwise pleasant, a needed vacation, and he enjoyed himself as much as possible, meeting a handful of Arthur's friends, riding through the colorful countryside with Arthur as his verbose tour guide, and eating at the more fashionable restaurants of the capitol in Santa Fe where they spent ten days.

Not a week after Eardley arrived he was moved to say, "Arthur, you have a magnificent start here. I am very impressed. Soon as I return to London I'll hold a meeting with our financial friends and proceed with raising investment capitol. It is yours as soon as you manage to secure the grant."

This was pleasing news to Arthur, and while Eardley was still in such an impressed state he hit him up for a thousand dollars, explaining how the building of his house and upgrading the grounds had strapped him some. Eardley could well understand that, yet was businessman enough to insist that Arthur sign a promissory note payable in five years at five percent interest. Arthur was pleased to do so. Later in August, the day before Eardley left for England, Arthur hit him up again, this time for a much greater sum. But the cautious capitalist in his older brother arose again to meet the challenge and sensibly took a mortgage on a large parcel of Arthur's property. When he accompanied Eardley shortly after to Raton where they pleasantly said their last goodbyes, neither realized that it would be the last time they ever would see each other again.

On 4 December 1899, the following year, Arthur obtained his United States citizenship papers at the Taos County Courthouse. He had applied once before in September 1883 in Raton, but never followed through. By doing so now he thought in practical terms of eliminating any possible future legal obstructions to his real estate ambitions. It was certainly an excellent idea, and a practical one at that.

With his new citizenship safely tucked under his arm, forty-year-old Arthur Rochford Manby began the new year of 1900 with a fresh feeling of purpose and confidence, zeal and direction. He would now continue carving out his future as an American, as a legal participant in this alien environment, and feel more secure. He would sharpen his ingenuity with the tools of whatever ingredients found around him, human or material, solid or nebulous, legal or non. He would continue determinedly upon his journey toward his dream, his empire. There was room for him here, he knew, for this country was rife with go-getters: Gould, Fisk, Carnegie and Rockefeller, to name but a few. Soon he would add the name Manby to the roster. Yes! He was the conquistador again, girding his loins, mounting his steed, armed with hubris, galloping off against the unwashed hordes of pagan peasantry, smoting and smiting right and left with his singing broadsword to claim what was rightfully his: a place in the conqueror's sun.

On this icy New Year's Day afternoon , he crunched through the crusty snow of his interior back yard on the way to the stables to check on his cows and draw some milk. He was suddenly halted in mid-step by a penetrating throb in his temple, more like a pulsating bruise. It was probably the cold air of the altitude, he winced, squeezing the side of his head to massage it deeply. Over the years he now and then came under the brief botheration, more an irritating intrusion really, but he would just as quickly forget about it as it faded, and continue on his way. He stood puzzled a moment, standing in his snow-blanketed yard, staring and wondering where he was, disorientated, suspended. Pained. A stranger in his own home, he stared at the adobe walls around him, everything a cipher, a blank. After a space of time he stirred, gradually regained his sense of presence, remembered who and where he was, then continued on his way to the barn.

Before the week was over he was out and about in his eager preying manner, cajoling and plaguing the small landowners of the grant in his usual undiplomatic style, using the weapons of threats and intimidation. He was more impatient than ever now, seeing them as objects impeding his destiny, and not humans surviving best they could in a perpetual day after day, hand-to-mouth existence. He saw in a flash of envy how the Maxwell people easily solved that problem by renting armed thugs to terrorize the undesirables off their acreage, and wished he could do the same. Recalling his brief "service" in Jim Masterson's Militia brought him a warm smile of delight, even though in the gunman's case he was shortly marched out of town by an aroused citizenry, a pistol-whipped, humiliated, peregrinating biped.

Yet the resistance from the occupiers against Manby's efforts grew. In his mind-set he did not realize that the heated abhorrence and hostility toward him was a reflection of his own obvious and blatant contempt toward them, his haughty "class" scorn which Arthur could not and would not hide nor disguise, even for the sake of trying to wrench the land from their grasp, his short suits being diplomacy and tact. His very presence to them was looked upon as a plague, and some even refused to speak to him, slamming their doors in his face as if he were the devil himself. He writhed against what he saw as undignified behavior. Worse yet, disrespect! He had to find a way to get them off "his" land.

Suddenly it came to him.

Since his identity was too well known now and reviled, he would work stealthily, from the shadows, surreptitiously. Clandestinely. Serpentine-like. A clandestine serpent, he grinned. He selected a trio of local lawyers to purchase what he could not. And he was cunning in his choice of legal beagles in that he selectively chose not only Hispanics, but strugglers in the craft not successful, barely able to keep their heads up economically. Capable, but not exceedingly bright; hungry and grateful for the work, but not overly greedy or inquisitive as to his purpose. And of course satisfied with the low wages he doled out. The three lawyers hopped about the grant like eager bunnies sniffing and chomping through a cabbage patch, wheedling and persuading the tenants to sell their parcels to them, and were quite successful. As they collected their wares, the more capable of the trio of cottontails, Antonio Gallegos, would trek down to Santa Fe weekly to turn over their work to an Anglo judge in his mid-fifties, Napoleon Bonaparte Laughlin, who would in turn sign over all the purchases to Manby. Arthur was smug over his cleverness. Yet it truly was a clever ploy, so why shouldn't he be appreciative of his ingenuity? He often laughed to himself, how the poor fools who sold to the badgering lawyers were blind to the outcome that they were actually in the end handing over their property to him. He was tempted to send each a thank-you note, wondering what the expression on their faces would be. He would love to have seen that. No, no, he chortled. Leave well enough alone.

But as favorable as things turned out he saw that he couldn't continue buying in small lots, a portion here, a portion there, for it would be too costly and he hadn't the money to invest in such a draining scheme. Also, a small group of owners clustered together to form a bloc against selling to anybody. Period. That insubordinate act increased both his ire and his determination no end. So again, he had to find a way. And then just as suddenly, it once more came to him. Ah, yes, quasi-legal, but workable.

What he would do is persuade the local county officials to reduce the land's value, and then he would pick it up for the taxes. In a letter to Laughlin on 23 May 1900, Manby spoke to him of his plan for perfect title, opening with a compliment to his silent partner.

"Dear Judge.

"I am much obliged for your prompt reply to mine of the twentieth. You devised just what I have in my mind, re final issue of tax suit ie perfect title. But the successful consummation of this, as you know, in a great measure depends on the skill and secrecy with which our moves are made, so that we shall not be held up by more plotters in unlooked-for quarters. And if we manage matters carefully and skillfully we shall have the grant title perfected before others realize what we are after.

"I am very anxious to get a copy of the (?) final grant, and would much appreciate your sending a copy together with expense entailed at your very earliest convenience, as I wish to send it to parties east.

"There is one more question I forgot to ask you. Namely, in case of a sale of the grant, will it be sold to the highest bidder without reserve—that is assuming that the costs (?) amounted to two thousand dollars. Could the grant be sold say for one thousand dollars, if this were the highest bid?

"As you probably know I hold all the interests of Mariano Sanches and his wife Maria del Rosario, with the exception of Gertrudis and (?) his five children, (?) whom Francisco Martinez inherited—though I have also deeds for a portion of this.

"So that if I (was) represented by A, hold the title, and B purchases the (?) title, between us we should get a good title at the end of three years.

"If you would express your views fully on this in your next it would help me by confirming to Eastern parties our modus operandi."

Leaving Lawyer Gallegos and Judge Laughlin to continue working their magic on the grant tenants, Manby left town.

Returning to Taos some seventeen months later, Arthur revealed in a letter to Laughlin on 7 October 1901.

"My dear Sir. I have recently returned from Old Mexico where I have been for nearly a year. I am anxious to know the status of the tax suit in the Antonio Martinez Grant.

"You will remember our former conversation, re, perfecting title and concluded that the easiest and safest way would be to have the grant sold for taxes after we had got the taxes reduced to as little as possible, and that you would appear & hold the case over until we were ready to take this business up. I am just in receipt of a letter from my friends in the East who are now prepared to go ahead and push this business. They represent large capitol and we all ought to make some money out of this transaction.

"I feel sure that I can depend on your help and cooperation in this important business. My friends are to be in Taos shortly, and after looking over the land, we expect to come to Santa Fe and avail ourselves of your services to accomplish this desired end.

"Hoping to have a profitable report from you as early as possible, thus I can show them to my friends on our stern resolve here.

"P.S. I have made a rough computation of taxes up to 1901, which might still be reduced, what do you think?"

There is some thought that his mentioned journey was not south to Mexico, but north to Colorado, specifically Edgewater, where he visited his brother Jocelyn.

Over the years Arthur claimed travels to a great number of cities for investment gathering forays, and name-dropped firms and companies like an ultra globe-trotting executive. Were they all actually legitimate physical contacts, or had he merely a handful of clever letter-writing ploys to build up a bogus resume with papered missives reflecting tomes of self-important queries and plans? To proudly and impressively display before prospective clients? And who were the interested "parties back East" he emphasized several times? The aroma of posturing is there, and if it were, who better to create the illusion of a hustling and masterful entrepreneur-promoter? Was it merely a game to give the impression of accumulated wealthy contacts in order to draw in the wide-eyed dupes who dreamed of sharing a bite from Arthur's plate of prosperity, who in the end would only be mercilessly separated from their money?

So, with Judge Laughlin as his Tonto, or Kato, or even Moe, Manby surged ruthlessly forward in his campaign to sweep away the stubborn holdouts from what he now perceived as his private domain. They were merely a school of small fish and Arthur Rochford Manby was dropping by for dinner. His vast knowledge of grant history, legalities, and territorial and federal law was deep and wide now, for he studied for years in order to understand its bounds, limitations and loopholes. He was a student preparing for his doctorate, earlier realizing he had better know what the waters were like he was diving into, and he prepared himself well. It all paid off, for no one in Taos could even think of matching his legal expertise, and he marched from official to official bombarding them with writs, suits and bills which left them dizzy and confused. The petit bureaucrates were of course no match for him, not only because of their limited perception of grant law, but nothing like this legal challenge had ever faced them before. Consequently, Arthur was able to cow them completely with his legal truncheons and papered petitions. If not a genius he was a step away, and although grudgingly, they held a great respect for his profound legal striding.

Even the sometimes unethical and calculating Laughlin had to give Manby a nod in that direction, for the Englishman left him in the dust. The judge himself had represented his share of land grant settlements, usually taking a third or a half of a grant as his fee. For his work on the Jacoma Grant he was refereed a third of it in 1909, approximately 2,300 acres. Exactly what arrangements the two made concerning the Martinez Grant is unknown, but whatever it was, one can be certain it never fell short of Arthur's wishes.

Frank Waters' biography of Arthur Manby, *To Possess the Land*, contains an incisive portrait of the Englishman in action, and at his best when dealing with a prey. It also seems that the ensnared Juan de los Reyes Santistevan and Arthur Manby were made for each other. Or perhaps Fate, bored, gave in to a sadistic streak to break the monotony.

Juan Santistevan at seventy-seven was a prosperous and noted

Taoseno who had for years enjoyed a successful mercantile career. He was descended from an old Spanish family and had the right to prefix his name with the Spanish title, "Don." He had served various offices such as postmaster, chairman of the school board, probate judge, state legislature and the senate. In short, he was an individual of professional and social stature in the community, a man of respect. Suddenly he came upon hard times and found himself in mounting debt. Somewhere, somehow, his financial obligations got the better of him. For a time he secured a series of bank loans as his stay-out-of-jail card. But it only slowed down the dark inevitable. Suddenly, his back was to the wall.

How well he knew Manby is speculative, but he was undoubtedly aware of this local bright sun of prosperity which shown lustrously throughout the area; his mining interests, properties and stories of sumptuous wealth. He believed too that Arthur Manby belonged to that fraternity of successful businessman, like him, and since that was the case, Juan felt the affluent Englishman would be sympathetic to his chaotic plight and be glad to help. Also, it was said Manby was seeing one of Juan's daughters, the young, budding, teenaged Celina. She was the last of six daughters available for marriage, although no word of a serious enough courtship was brought up between the two.

But Juan's wife Doña Maria was not too enthralled with his going to Manby for help, nor was she too enthused over their headstrong daughter being seen in his company, feeling the old man was compromising the family name. Actually, she thought him a scoundrel. Further, she realistically doubted there would be any kind of marriage on the horizon between the old coot and Celina. But Juan's troubles were financial, not domestic, and he set his priorities accordingly. And what did women know of high finance and business, anyway? The home was their domain, he tired of telling her. The kitchen and marital duties.

So Santistevan sought Manby out, and after a long discussion of trustingly opening his painful problem to him, Arthur smiled with eyes glistening which Juan mistook for sincere concern.

"Juan," confided Arthur. "There is a simple answer. Easy as pie."

This was the best news Santistevan could ever have hoped for, and his heart burst with gladness. Arthur went on and warmly explained that he must file bankruptcy instantly and turn over all his holdings to him. Lemminglike and without question, Juan did as he was told.

Why this businessman so blindly and voluntarily immerse himself deeper into the black abyss of no return is another Taos mystery. On Saturday, 7 June 1902, the newspaper *La Revista De Taos* announced: "ASSIGNATION. Don Juan Santistevan, Sr., prominent rancher and land owner, has assigned his holdings to Mr. A.R. Manby for the benefit of his creditors. The total listing is as follows: Approximately 20,000 sheep and lambs valued at $30,000. About 75,000 pounds of wool, $9,750. Assets and merchandise in his store, $30,000. Bookeeping, obligations and securities, $15,000. All real estate (less home residence), $15,000. Total, $99,750.00."

In the column to the left and next to Santistevan's financial listing is the unsurprising item, "Judge N.B. Laughlin arrived from Santa Fe Tuesday to serve as 'devil's advocate' for A.R. Manby, whom Don Juan Santistevan appointed financial arbiter of his estate."

He then closed his bank account and sat back, awaiting his future son-in-law to save him.

But alas, instead of a life preserver Arthur handed him a rock of prodigious size, and with it clutched to his breast Don Juan de los Reyes Santistevan sank to total economic oblivion. Briefly, Arthur had a few of his cronies appraise Juan's stock to rock-bottom prices. Manby then put all his holdings up for sale, turned around and purchased them through dummy fronts, and sold everything at a juicy profit. He evicted Santistevan's married daughters and families from their homes to sell their houses. One daughter and husband he sued for $6,758.96, but ended taking four pieces of property in settlement. Arthur and his devil's advocate had done a thorough job.

Santistevan, now shamed and penniless and ruined beyond repair, took his broken and demoralized self home and wondered what hit him. On 21 August 1908, he quietly surrendered the last asset he possessed on earth, his life.

It was a few years before this when Manby was described as slipping into an out-of-control rage which nearly ended in homicide. On Saturday morning, 26 November 1904, as he was passing the restaurant of the Columbian Hotel on the plaza, he saw through the bay window the man he had of late become side-wise with. Arthur without hesitation entered the eatery and moved swiftly toward his target who was breakfasting and conversing with a male companion. The man fortunately spied him in time and in alarm half-rose to meet him. Manby slashed at him with his knife but was able only to cut the wrist of one of his hands upraised in self-defense.

The recipient of Arthur's fury was twenty-seven-year-old Taos newspaper editor Jose Montaner. Of French ancestry but born in Barcelona, Spain in 1877, the educated and cultured Montaner emigrated to the United States, and in 1901 was in Taos as editor of *La Revista De Taos* (The Review of Taos), a Spanish language paper of some 5,000 subscribers.

In 1905, he would marry Mariquita Valdez, and in 1912 would be appointed Taos County Superintendent of Schools. During his term he saw to the building of forty-some schools, including the first high school of Taos. Eventually he won election to the state legislature. As an added side-note, Montaner claimed descent from the noted rebel cleric of Taos, Padre Antonio Jose Martinez. The Catholic Priest owned the first printing press in the area upon which he printed its first newspaper in 1834, *El Crepusculo De Libertad* (The

Dawn of Liberty). In irony, roughly sixty-seven years later Montaner was the editor of that paper's descendent, *La Revista*.

But now here he sat clutching his bleeding wrist following being attacked by a riotously distempered Arthur Manby. Fortunately for the editor his breakfast partner, State Senator Ramon Sanchez, delayed not a moment. He quickly stood, grabbed a nearby chair, and clubbed Manby over the head, felling him to the floor. Within moments the groggy assailant was able to regain his feet to flee out the door and away from the scene.

That Saturday's edition of *La Revista* carried a short column concerning the affair beneath the banner, !ATENCION!, and described the bout. It stated, "Mister Montaner was a victim of another criminal act against his life on Saturday morning when he was eating his lunch (sic). A man by the name of A.R. Manby attacked him from behind like a cowardly assassin, a man who lacks the qualities of a gentleman. He was beaten, hurt, and left unconscious.

"Mister Montaner finds himself in terrible pain and is under the care of Doctor Cook.

"Manby assaulted Mister Montaner without any warning or exchange of words. People are ignorant as to motives.

"The authorities are investigating the matter."

Editor Jose Montaner's account of the melee in his deposition of 7 December 1904, somewhat echoes the *La Revista* column. He claimed that while breakfasting Arthur Manby hit him from behind without warning, "in a brutal and cruel manner, striking this plaintiff on the head, face and other parts of the body thereby causing concussion of the brain and a compound fracture of one nasal bone and lacerating three of the plaintiff's fingers by forcibly drawing plaintiff's table knife through his hand, whereby plaintiff was made ill and disabled from attending to business for five days thereafter, to his damage in the sum Five Hundred ($500.00) Dollars." The editor also asserted, "He was confined to his bed for five days thereafter suffering greatly in both body and mind, and for about Twenty-Four Hours of said five days was in a semi-conscious state."

In conclusion, Montaner prayed judgment against Manby for $500 for assault and battery, $200 for special damages, and one hundred dollars for exemplary damages.

In Manby's deposition of 16 February 1905 is his account of the confrontation, and it differs quite considerably. According to him the inevitable clash between the two men had been heating up for more than six months. Arthur claimed during all that time Montaner published false and slanderous statements about him in his paper, *La Revista*. Additionally, he said the editor on occasion publically insulted him grossly in a bantering, threatening manner. He further spoke of a close crony of the editor's, Esteven Sanchez, who intended on doing Manby physical harm.

On the morning of their quarrel Arthur entered the Columbian Hotel's dining room and sat at a breakfast table occupied by two other men. Almost immediately, Jose Montanter and Esteven Sanchez seated themselves at the same table and began conversing brusquely with Manby. Arthur protested their presence, but the duo continued their verbalizing more aggressively toward him, "in a gross, vulgar, indecent and threatening manner."

When again Manby complained, that they cease their conduct and leave, having his fill of their scurrilous verbosity, Sanchez became even more pointedly insulting toward the Englishman. At this moment Arthur "did then and there strike said Sanchez and then and there with one blow put him, the said Sanchez out of action, and with his open hand slap said plaintiff (Montaner) on one side of his head and cautioned him to be quiet and desist from any further assaults and threats, whereupon the said plaintiff struck defendant (Manby) on the chest with his table knife, and he (Manby) was compelled to take the knife from the hand of the plaintiff by force to protect and defend himself." Manby claimed this was the limit of the force he had used to defend himself.

Oddly, neither the newspaper item nor Montaner's deposition make mention of the editor's "breakfast of champions" chair-wielder, Esteven Sanchez, or of "Senator Ramon Sanchez." Strange too, neither presence was noted by Montaner, especially following his dramatic, chair-clubbing role. Arthur's heated mindset over the entire affair is visibly evident in his determined signature at the end of his deposition. It sat heavy and serrated with picket-fenced, shark's-teeth slashes, leaning strongly rightward, straight across the bottom of the sheet, the tail of the final "Y" of his name swung in a downward knife sweep to the left in a single long stroke, a sword-thrust emphasis to his challengers. It seemed more an announcement than a signature, declaiming that when aroused he was not a man to toy with.

Arthur's defending attorney throughout the proceedings was his partner in the on-going Martinez Grant takeover/buyout, Judge Napoleon Bonaparte Laughlin.

Following the brief, violent collision, Manby left the hotel for his home. It was near ten in the morning. Along the way, as he was passing Holder's Saloon, he met two men, Agapito Martinez and William L. McClure. They would later be witnesses for editor Montaner, and on 8 June 1925, gave the following depositions of their meeting with Manby. (Minor punctuation corrections for clarity.)

"He was talking about having hit Montaner," spoke Martinez to his interrogator.

"Repeat just what and all he said about the plaintiff as near as you can," was the questioner's reply.

"I and McClure, we started to Mr. McClure's house, and Mr. Manby walked together with us, to (in) the direction of Mr. McClure's house. On the road where we were going he showed us one of his hands all swelled up and some scratches on the back of his hand, and I asked him, what he had (hit with) that hand, and he answered me that it was on account of the stroke he gave Montaner, and I told him why did you not prosecute him according to law? He told me he was instructed by some of the officials of Santa Fe, that the best way to fix these Spaniards was to hit them."

McClure in his turn said, "He was talking about his trouble with Montaner."

"Repeat just what and all he said about the plaintiff as near as you can," replied the interrogator.

"First he showed me the back of his hand, the one he hit Mr. Montaner with which was swelled considerable. Then as I had some business with Mr. Martinez at my house I suggested to Mr. Martinez that he walked (sic) up to the house with me. He started and Mr. Manby walked along between us. On the way to my house which is about two blocks from Holder's Saloon, Manby enter (sic) into conversation in Spanish, about the trouble he had that morning with Montaner, that Montaner had spoken disrespectfully of some ladies of Manby's acquaintance, also that he had been advised by some officials of Santa Fe to assault Montaner. This is the substance of the conversation to my best recollection."

It also seems Manby made no mention to them of Esteven Sanchez or his striking him, nor the identities of the Santa Fe officials who gave him the advice to assault the editor.

Exactly what Montaner printed in the *Revista* concerning Manby is unknown. But there is a thought he may have continually and abrasively criticized the rapacious and repugnant manner in which Manby was collecting the properties on the Martinez Grant, allowing his passion to steer him into dangerous waters. In addition, Manby about this time had by now divested himself of Santisteven's properties, and Montaner may have called him on it and his appalling methodology, furiously feeling further laundering concerning his unethical practices was more than appropriate. But of course the brickbats were lost on the Englishman, for although he took the criticism as a personal insult, he also ignored them possibly thinking turning the other cheek would dull the editor's pen and turn his interest elsewhere. Was Montaner justified in his editorializing? Most certainly, and as both, an editor and private citizen. He would be remiss if he did not at least raise questions. Yet his methods were as indelicate and tactless as Manby's. Thus, Montaner's crusading pen scribbled on, leaden with equal amounts of Don Quixote and malice, finally reaping the Englishman's wrath.

It had been commented upon that Montaner had a careless tendency to be somewhat rash or hasty in his printed comments and opinions. Perhaps his emotions had the upper hand on certain issues and without cool-headed self-editing he tossed rocks too freely and undiplomatically, using a hammer instead of a scalpel. Possibly this tendency of his is what may have ultimately culminated in the Columbian Hotel rumble. This literary looseness of his got him into extremely deep difficulty hardly a month earlier, on 29 November, when Taos County Sheriff Faustin Truillo, enraged and in a firestorm of fury, sued, served and arrested the editor for criminal libel. Perhaps this is what the earlier mentioned *La Revista* column was referring to when it spoke self-servingly of his being "a victim of another criminal attack." Sheriff Truillo's ranting charges stated that "...Jose Montaner in a vile and cowardly manner ... unlawfully did print and publish false, wicked, malicious and scandalous libel...."

Loose lips may sink ships, as the World War II bromide cautioned, but by the same token, loose pens often become double-edged swords.

Due to missing documents, a common occurrence in researching old records (such as the lost depositions of Montaner's other four witnesses, Dr. J.O. Cook, M.M. Pooler, Esteven Sanchez and A. Scheurich), a complete picture of events is difficult to describe, yet enough paperwork is on hand to create a fair idea. Also, were the above mentioned Pooler and Scheurich the two other men at the breakfast table fight that angry morning?

Manby's attorney, N.B. Laughlin, motioned to quash the depositions of Martinez and McClure on legal technicalities. Whether he was successful isn't known.

On 17 May 1905, a motion for a change of venue was made by Manby's attorney, ". . . because the inhabitants of said county of Taos are prejudiced against him. . . ." Also, results unknown.

Finally it appears the editor threw in the towel, for on 14 May 1907, the two arrived at a common solution. "It is hereby agreed and stipulated by and between the parties to this suit that the plaintiff (Montaner) shall and hereby does enter a dismissal of said cause, and defendant (Manby) agrees to such dismissal, upon the following grounds and stipulations:

"That the plaintiff and defendant shall each pay his own witnesses their fees, and that the balance of the court costs shall be divided and paid equally by each plaintiff and defendant."

Hostilities having ceased, the armistice was agreed upon and signed by both parties. The three-year war waged between the two antagonists now ended.

Yet, while in the trenches of his court fight Arthur did not allow himself to be deterred from his main goal, the acquisition of the Martinez Grant. With Judge Laughlin in the cheering section of the Colosseum of Questionable Proceedings, Manby led the campaign dauntlessly. Together they hatched a clever scheme of reevaluating the grant taxes to a lower scale, and Arthur harassed the county officials mercilessly. Many were hack-appointees, awarded their jobs via political favoritism, and not chosen for their positions because of experience or qualification. Thus, it worked in Manby's favor, for they were prime meals for the Englishman's jungle appetite, and easily daunted.

Arthur picked up 9,200 acres on 27 May 1903, for $36.11 in delinquent taxes. It was such a steal that deputy treasurer Henry Gonzales couldn't help but protest, albeit meekly, and Manby firmly reminded him he was paying the legal and asking price of the judgment stipulated. After court costs of $16.88, it totaled $52.99. Before long, another chunk of 6,200 acres was up for county sale at $126.25, again for back taxes. Desiring a touch of invisibility this time, shadowy Arthur induced a front-man to claim it for him, Antonio C. Pacheco of Arroyo Seco. These last two basement-bargains of a mere $179.24 made up in size over one-fourth of the grant. At this doleful news the handful of holdouts led by Daniel Martinez at long last threw in their cards in frustration and surrendered, selling out to Manby, the game being over. Awesome Arthur had finally done it. In a legal position now to declare ownership, he filed suit for quiet title on 6 October 1905. The grant was now practically his, and the triumph was exhilarating. He had but to wait patiently now for the final decree of conveyance at a future court hearing, to him merely a thing of formality.

Although Arthur was busy as a beaver manifesting his dream of building a real estate empire, he never forgot the possibility of striking it rich in the gold country, namely amid the copper-bearing fields and streams of Colfax County, approximately thirty miles northeast of Taos. Since the strike in 1867, thousands of miners were drawn to the region for years, and occasionally Manby made his own solitary and untrumpeted forays along the slopes of Mount Baldy. In 1897, on its northwestern side, he picked up the Golden Era claim from Thomas Clouser on 27 February, located at the head of Mills Gulch. Clouser discovered it back on 18 October 1895, and it was thought to be "one of the most promising claims in the Moreno District." How true that was and how much Manby paid for it is unknown, but in late 1899 Arthur sold the Golden Era (also called the War Eagle, the Twinn, and the Fairfax Mines), to Judge M.R. Baker and other Elizabeth Town individuals for $900. Ambitiously, the Judge and his associates incorporated the Golden Era Mining and Milling Company with the backing of Missouri and eastern stockholders. Up through 1901, a considerable amount of labor and cost was inflicted upon the mine but it all turned out to be a lackluster and unprofitable venture. Why the earlier boastful promises failed to surface is shrouded in the mists of mining history. It may possibly all the while have been PR hyperbole.

The stories of the discovery of the gold on 12,441-foot Mount Baldy in 1866 are somewhat conflicting and varied. Blanche Chloe Grant, novelist and some-time resident of Taos in the 1920s and early 1930s, describes a Ute or Apache bringing a beautiful stone of green and blue to Fort Union to trade. Two of the men, recognizing it for what it was, copper, "thought it wise to act immediately and dispatched one of their fellows with the Indian, somewhat richer in pocket, to find the place from which the stone had come. Straight to the ridge of Baldy they went and a mine was located and marked."

The History of New Mexico somewhat echoes Grant, but adds that after viewing the rock, "William Kroenig, W.H. Moore and others around the fort became interested. After paying the Indian for his information, they sent a man with him to locate the find, and the two proceeded directly to the top of Baldy where an abundance of copper ore was found. This trip resulted in what was known for years afterward as the 'Copper Mine' or the 'Mystic Lode.'"

Lawrence Murphy also speaks of soldiers who became interested in the greenish-blue rocks Utes and Apaches brought down from Baldy Mountain. "One curious soldier climbed high atop Baldy to a place where he found the slopes blanketed with what he knew to be copper float and laid out a claim to what became the Mystic Lode or Copper Mine."

Jim Berry Pearson told of Utes and Apaches who "occasionally exchanged goods with the soldiers at Fort Union. In 1866, an Indian showed some 'pretty rock' he had found to Captain William H. Moore, William Kroenig, and others at the fort, which they immediately recognized as a rich copper float. . . . They induced the Indian to lead them to the spot where he had found the multicolored specimen. He guided Moore and his party to the top of Baldy, where such an abundance of ore was evident that they quickly located the 'Copper Mine.'"

Some narratives append the account with an appreciative Native turning up at Fort Union with some "pretty rocks" to give to Captain Moore. It was said the gift was a heartfelt gesture toward Moore after he found a badly wounded and dying tribesman in the mountains, whom Moore humanely brought to the Fort Union hospital for treatment, saving his life. Further, the Native donor and his companions were only too glad to guide Moore and his party to its source up the slopes of Baldy.

Captain William Hubert Moore was a member of the California Column, a mixed cavalry-infantry organization roughly two thousand three hundred strong, commanded by Colonel James Henry Carleton. One year into the Civil War it was ordered in April 1862 to New Mexico Territory to assist in the repulsion of threatening Confederate incursions in the southwest. After their arrival in Santa Fe in September, and finding the Rebels had withdrawn their handful of forces back to the interior of Texas, Carleton's men were used in fighting and suppressing the various Amerind tribes throughout New Mexico and Arizona Territories wherever needed. A detachment was left for a time at Fort Union, and it wasn't too long before the gold-seeking appetites of several of the men were whetted, many being ex-miners from the gold fields of California. A local Native had brought in some "pretty rock" which turned out to be copper float.

As a result of the earlier mentioned Captain Moore party's discovery of the field of copper, upon their return to Fort Union three California Column men were dispatched to Mount Baldy to assess the area further. They were Lawrence F. Bronson, Peter Kinsinger, and Pat Kelley. Arriving on Willow Creek after a fifty-some mile journey, the men paused. It was a late October evening and the trio decided to make camp on the creek bank for the night, then proceed up Baldy in the morning. As Bronson and Kinsinger prepared supper, in the waning light Kelley thought he would check out the gravel along the stream's edge. He immediately panned out colors of gold, and continued to do so. His shouts of excitement drew his two companions, and supper was instantly a thing of the past, as was their scouting of Baldy. The trio worked feverishly for several days. Then, since it was late in the season, plus lacking the proper equipment for placer mining, they called it quits. Marking the large pine tree over their camp "discovery tree," they returned to Fort Union.

The group also vowed to keep silent over their discovery, probably speaking of it only to Moore, and return that spring. But as usual in cases of sworn silence a leak occurs, and before the snows of winter even melted, it was said many overly-impatient enthusiasts made the trek to the Baldy area despite the snow to look the place over. By spring of April and May 1867, a deluge of hopeful miners commenced to blanket the valley and all its many streams and creeks.

Exactly when Columbus Ferguson, William Stone, and Frank E. Wilkinson hit the lavish gold fields is unknown. One story related by Ferguson is that he discovered the Mystic and later took Stone in as his partner. The other version is that Stone discovered the Mystic and later took Ferguson as a partner. According to novelist Blanche Chloe Grant, writing in 1934, "Over thirty years ago (Ferguson) located the vein of copper which those earlier men of Fort Union failed to find and he named his mine the Mystic Lode. Then he cast about for partners. Two men stood ready to go in with him. 'I soon realized I had two greenhorns,' said Ferguson. 'Wilkinson slid off an alfalfa stack back in Kansas, and Stone, a Pennsylvania German, had worked in a soap factory in Cincinnati, I believe. They didn't know anything about mining. They didn't even know how to pack lumber on burros. After a year or so, each thought he was an expert miner.'

"'We packed the ore down on burros and had it arrasted (sic) and then sent the amalgam on to Denver. Lucien Maxwell (claiming ownership of the minefields), sent some copper clear across the plains by ox teams to Westport but we sent ours to Colorado. Later we shipped to El Paso.'" Ferguson at the time displayed a slip of paper dated 6 October 1913 denoting $1,950 for a carload of copper.

Ferguson and Stone were also partners in the Ajax Mine, not two miles south. Realistically, both mines were probably discovered earlier by others, and after depleted, sold, or abandoned. Then, when Wilkinson became the third partner of the Mystic and Ajax, things began to turn cloudy. About three years later Stone turned up dead, some say found frozen in the snow where he had supposedly lain all night. It occurred, some say, after Manby joined the trio. Others say Stone's demise happened earlier, following Wilkinson's joining the company. Now, in the early 1900s, the three associates Ferguson, Wilkinson, and Manby, were partners in the Mystic and Ajax Mines.

Later, detective Bill Martin in his report unsentimentally describes the trio. "Manby was the brain power, the writer of letters. He conducted not only the mining business but all legal matters." He had the reputation of knowing international as well as domestic law, particularly mining laws, more "than five other lawyers combined." Wilkinson was a clever and experienced crook. His expertise was in high-grading, stealing gold from whatever mines he worked in. Ferguson was the cold-blooded killer, "with murder in his eyes and heart." No Lavender Hill Mob there.

Manby often visited Columbus from time to time, especially earlier when the little family lived in Valdez, a small village in a scenic canyon north of Taos perhaps ten miles. On a cool summer Sunday in August 1902, he decided to ride out. It was a day when he experienced an unforgettable emotional encounter which seared and skewered his life ever after.

Columbus Ferguson was standing in the sun just outside his doorway with his wife and two girls as Manby rode up.

"Arthur, you old rascal," he laughed good-naturedly. "Good to see you!"

"And you too, Columbus!"

"You remember my daughters, Francesca and Terecita? Say Hello to the man, girls. It's Terecita's birthday today. She's fourteen."

Francesca, sixteen, stretched out a tiny hand with a shy smile, emitting a barely perceptive greeting. But it was Terecita, who stood silently gazing into Manby's eyes with a dark, smoky glare, who instantly mesmerized him. Arthur next extended his hand to acknowledge her own, which still hung at her side. Both girls were tiny and doll-like, lovely reflections of each other, slender and nubile, wielding the promise of future heart-breakers in the making. It had been several years since he had seen Terecita, and the change in her to him was miraculous. Something within the young girl reached out and smote him. Arthur literally melted beneath her ebony agates as he slid back in time, transformed slowly and imperceptibly into a forty-three-year-old teenager, callow and clumsy, confused and emotionally asea. No woman in his life had ever touched him like this. Terecita calculatingly let him feel foolish with his hand stuck out overly-long in mid air, a fisherman without a pole, and when she finally took his hand it was with more of a caress than a shake. The thought struck him she was no young girl, that she had within her an old heart. There was old blood in her, seers would say. She was an old soul, others would claim. Arthur caught another vision, and in one glance he was completely captivated: fata morgana. Her obsidian orbs of deep ebony and wavy raven tresses shown glowingly in the sun as she purred in perfect English with an enticing smile, "Hello, Mister Manby."

He stood before her helplessly gazing upon her fey beauty, feeling lost, and then found, as if awakening from a long sleep.

Unbelievable. She appeared before him as a young princess. Yes. Shakespeare's line, "Who has seen the mobled Queen?" thundered in his brain.

As their guest that night, Arthur as usual spread his blanket and slept on the floor, a restless slumber to be sure. His head was filled with whimsical wishes and unbelievable adventures of the heart, seeing himself at one turn grasping the grail, and on the other an old fool blind to reality.

In the chilled morning as Arthur mounted to ride off he smiled down at Columbus and said, "That charming slip of a girl of yours, Terecita. A princess if there ever was one. Tell her I look forward to seeing her again. She is enchanting, Columbus! Devastatingly enchanting!"

With a wave and a giddy laugh Manby trotted away, and as he looked back a moment he spied his princess standing in the open doorway in a short, diaphanous shift, barefooted, her tiny hand up in a little flutter, Mona Lisa smile and all. More sorceress than child. His heart did a tumble while a whimper caught his throat, and he was lost again. This old counterfeiter of bogus schemes and this wisp of a teen who had the awareness of her unnatural impact upon certain men, bonded immediately. It was the most profound experience in Arthur's life, his sword-in-the-stone event, his tumbling from a jackass on the way to Damascus. It was a numbing, perceptive-altering phenomenon. Fata morgana? More fatal morgana, actually.

After becoming a third wheel in the Mystic and Ajax, Manby traveled much as his grant business allowed to the western slope mines, staying with the Fergusons for a week or two at a time in Elizabethtown. The town was five miles west of Mount Baldy, and although no longer the county seat, the honor having passed on to Cimarron, then Springer, and finally to Raton in 1897, it yet housed a goodly, although diminishing, population. With each visit Arthur brought gifts for the children, especially Terecita, whom he doted upon constantly and called "his little princess." His enthrallment over her was not lost on Columbus, who saw in it more as a convenient binding process, a cat's-paw which kept Manby close to the bosom of their business arrangement. It cemented the fixated pawn and his vaunted wealth and influence as a fly to honey, making him a valued member of the tiny trio in their nefarious schemes. No, he would not shoo this heel-fly away for they needed him dearly. The three were a neat and tidy package as far as Columbus was concerned, and if they were careful they would profit greatly for a few years to come with no one suspecting what they were about.

High-grading, the theft of gold from mines, was a perpetual curse to owners and managers the world over. While a tasty occasional sideline to some, it was a profitable profession to others; while some practitioners looked upon it as a craft, to the more adept it was an art. But whatever and however it was rationalized and justified by the various specialists, all were looked upon as maggots on the profession by the mine owners and a constant drain on their profits. Wilkinson was a high-grading artist, and he and Ferguson would work in an assortment of mines to practice their villainous talents.

The Mystic sat near the southwestern cap of Baldy at perhaps 12,300 feet, while the Ajax was a little under two miles directly south, at about 8,000 feet. Both mines were barren now and considered unproductive—except perhaps for a piece of mineral "discovered" now and then to give the rumor of a new awakening. Both shafts were now used as a front. While Ferguson and Wilkinson hired out to other mines in the area, some close, such as the juicy Legal Tender, just to the northeast of the Ajax, but especially the richest and most pilfered of all, the Aztec—conveniently located on the opposite side of the mountain from the Mystic a tad under two miles—the Ajax and Mystic were used as handy caching sites. The most important was the Ajax, where the booty was stored in sacks and hidden. When enough was accumulated, they were shipped out every six months or so via burro to El Paso by Wilkinson to a contact man who paid him off, and who then took the plunder to Mexico. It actually was a sweet arrangement, and of course profitable, risky as it also was.

Perhaps their earlier partner Stone was killed because he was a threat to the scheme. While Wilkerson and Ferguson enthusiastically put the idea together, they may have found the fly in the ointment was Stone. He may have wanted nothing to do with the arrangement, may have even been horrified by it, being an honest man, that other rare specimen on the slopes and streams. Too, he may have vowed to expose the pair to the mining authorities, and if so, had sealed his doom.

Jim Berry Pearson in his unpublished thesis has interesting and enlightening information on many mines in the Baldy area, and his commentaries on several may serve a purpose here as to the possible machinations and movements of the Manby-Ferguson-Wilkinson troika. The two digs which concerns the story here are the Legal Tender and the Ajax, both a stone's throw across Willow Creek from each other. Both accounts are worth quoting in full. First is the Legal Tender.

"The old Legal Tender, long listed as one of the best prospects in the field, was naturally one of the Willow Creek District properties to attract capitalists. In the fall of 1896, a group of Kansas men decided that this mine was the one with which to gain a fortune in gold. Since the values had proven so satisfactory, they concluded that the only drawback to successful operations was the lack of milling facilities. By the end of November, preparations were being made to erect a twenty-ton Huntington mill in Grouse Gulch; a force of men was immediately set to work building roads to the selected site. The labor was carried on with such vigor that the mill was in operation and producing gold by the end of March 1897. On 5 June, the proprietors, A. Clauson, A.C. Majors, W.P. McDonald, John W. Williams, all of Elizabethtown, A.C. Woodwin of Kansas City, Mo.,

G.W. Goldman of Kansas City, and J.W. Sherlock of Emporia, Kan., incorporated the Legal Tender Mining Company for $500,000.

"Throughout the fall of 1897, the Legal Tender miners worked veins from six to ten feet wide, assaying from twenty-five to two hundred dollars in gold. A.C. Major announced the following fall that he would operate the mill on other ores in the district and enough men accepted his offer to keep it running full blast. Both mill and mine were operated steadily throughout 1899, but the yields were not up to expectations. To correct the situation, the company decided to add a cyanide treating process. With the additional backing of some Chicago men, excavations were begun by the new superintendent, O.F. Matkin of Chicago, early in January 1900. Little work was completed on the project during the spring of 1900, but a strike early that May on ore assaying $500 per ton convinced the company that the cyanide process would surely pay. Matkin hurried to Denver for the machinery. The five-ton cyanide mill was ready for operation by the end of June, but to the owner's horror, the process would not separate the gold from the Legal Tender ores.

"The Legal Tender company men had quite an investment in their property by the end of 1900, and were not inclined to abandon it without another effort. Besides the Huntington mill and cyanide annex, a 650-foot gravity tramway, a complete assay office, a superintendent's house, and boarding houses and bunkhouses for the employees had been built. A gasoline engine hoist had been installed on a newly completed cross-cut tunnel. The workings consisted of over 700 feet on the vein, with fully as many more feet in cross-cuts and drifts. The vein was well-defined, cutting the entire formation, and carrying values from thirty to seventy-five dollars. Matkin put two shifts in the tunnels that December after hitting a lead running seventy-five dollars per ton. The Legal Tender was shut down from the middle of January 1902 to that June, and then pushed vigorously the remainder of the year. By 1903, the Legal Tender Mining

Company decided to call it quits; about $10,000, produced by the Huntington mill, was its total return and costs were piling up. Under new management a new tunnel was started at the foot of the hill in February 1904, but work stopped that May and the old mine remained silent."

And now next we hear from the Ajax.

"Just as active as the Legal Tender mine during these years was the Ajax claim adjoining it to the south. It was discovered by J.A. Wolcott in April 1889—but not filed until September 28, 1894, and very little work was done until 1895. By the end of 1895, a tunnel penetrating the claim for about seventy feet had hit ore that tested well—so well that Wolcott was able to secure financial backing. The Golden Ajax Mining Company was organized in February 1896 with Jacob King president; J.A.Wolcott, vice president; W.B. Ferris, treasurer; C.R. Slusser, secretary; and who all together with Clay R. Hall comprised the owners, operators and directors. Already, these men had ordered the machinery for a ten-stamp mill costing $4,000. Stacked on the dumps awaiting completion of the mine was 5,000 tons of ore.

"On 27 May 1896, the Ajax mill blew its first whistle and commenced pounding ore at the rate of about fifteen tons per day. A three-day test yielded $400 worth of gold; the company was so pleased that more lumber was ordered for improving the property. The mill was run night and day, averaging twelve dollars per ton. Company officers talked seriously about enlarging it another ten stamps and adding a concentrator. By the end of the summer it was reported that the Golden Ajax Company was taking out about $100 worth of gold daily. The jubilant stockholders threw a big dance in Elizabethtown to celebrate their good fortune.

"The Ajax mine and mill were operated throughout the winter of 1896-1897 despite heavy snows. A shortage of wood and the inability to bring in further supplies due to the condition of the roads caused a temporary shutdown, however, in March 1897. Development continued throughout the summer and fall, with the yield running from fifteen to twenty dollars per ton. During 1898 the production began to fall far below expenses. J.O. Dimmick, an expert mill man from Denver, was employed by Manager Harvey Finch to remodel the mill, and A.C. McLeod of Denver took charge of operations that December. The miners still failed to find free-milling ores which could be treated successfully in a stamp mill, and after a few runs the Ajax was in the "red." The property was placed in the hands of trustees during 1899, and some development was done for them by C.C. Forrester the following spring.

"C.C. Forrester took a year's bond from the trustees of the Golden Ajax in December 1900 for $14,400. Ore was shipped to the Black Copper mill during the spring of 1901 to see how well it could be treated by the cyanide process. After runs yielding from fifteen to over twenty-dollars had been made, Forrester praised the Black Copper highly and indicated that he would put in such a mill. The reason for his loss of interest is not known, but he failed to take up the bond and the Ajax mine and mill were bonded and leased to O.F. Matkin. It was still considered one of the best mines in the field, with large bodies of ore carrying values from eight to ten dollars per ton. In addition to the mill, equipped with two batteries of five stamps each, a Blake crusher, automatic feeders, and a fifty horse-power boiler and engine, there were bunk and boarding houses for the men. The mine and mill were both operated for a time during the summer of 1902, but Matkin like his predecessors, found that the ores could not be treated profitably by the stamp machine. The Ajax was worked intermittently during the next three years, and though there is no record of the yield, it was estimated as being negligible."

As many mines played out over the years and became infertile holes in the ground, they were deserted by their owners who often packed up and moved on to look for fresh diggings elsewhere.

Consequently, the abandoned claims became tax delinquent, and every summer were sold off at sheriff's sales. Was this the opportunity Ferguson and Wilkinson took advantage of, picking up the Ajax and Mystic for a pittance and using them as a blind, as storing facilities for their pillaged plunder from other mines? The situation was ideally suited for the two conspirators, and it was a perfect stratagem for them to carry out their ambitious aim of "topping off" wealth from other men's investments. And with Manby as their third wheel, would he not have been only too happy to contribute to the scheme by furnishing the sums as needed in purchasing the now sterile claims, and any equipment necessary?

As Ferguson and Wilkinson plied their talents over the many hills and arroyos of the Mount Baldy region, Manby too wasted no time. For starters, he organized and chartered the Taos Valley Land Company on 24 April 1905. On the board of five directors were Manby and good old Judge Laughlin. The three others were unwitting stockholders from Michigan, Missouri and Minnesota. Awash in the euphoria of accomplishment, Arthur proudly mounted the company sign on the front of his adobe wall. Yes, he was on his way! He then cranked out a tome of letters to the east coast and England, enticing money from whomever and wherever he could, trumpeting and hyperbolizing his planned development of the grant, and was surprisingly successful. Even Eardley came through with a monied client, a young woman of Ireland, Margaret Higgins. Although his predatory style was nothing short of baited thievery, he must have possessed enough of the method actor, coupled with his cock-sure chutzpah, to draw the needed investors he sought. He then eagerly hit the road eastward, for that is the direction quite correctly where the biggest bundles of green was to be found. On the wide canvas of his imagination he painted colorful scenes of his intent for the potential investors, a modern pied-piper drawing hapless hopefuls into the quicksands of his boggy minefield.

Yet, Arthur's heralding of his plans for the grant was truly impressive and ambitious. His agenda was to encourage the immigration of an industrious population for the purpose of creating colonies and communities throughout its vast landscape. Its potential lay in the land itself with some coal and salts (and like a good salesman he touched upon the possibilities of gold mines), but more realistically it lay in the areas of cultivating a variety of crops and orchards, the raising and breeding of livestock—cattle, horses, sheep and goats—the laying out of roads and streets, power and gas plants, lighting and telephone lines, and the eventual presence of a railroad. Within the sprouting villages and towns would mushroom a myriad of shops and stores and businesses, creating a trading climate which would encourage and foster growth and economic strength for the entire plat. It was a worthy dream for any developer-capitalist, and perhaps in the hands of a more practical and focused planner-financier it may have actually happened. But somewhere, somehow, and for some reason Arthur's plans sadly never went much beyond the stage of dreams, schemes and depictive verbiage. Was it all glib verbosity of smoke and mirrors in order to merely enrich himself, with no real thought of building anything except his personal bank account? Or was he actually stymied when it came to the realistic part of his dream, that he was unable to carry it to fruition for the lack of having practical vision? Could he but dream and not build? Was he a man who could draw a house but was helpless in the use of a hammer and nail?

If it were possible to sift and examine the archaeology of Arthur's heart, brain and soul perhaps some answers to his behavior could be found, a reason or two grasped, or a more solid hypothesis arrived at. But alas, little is known of his background and personal life but bits and bytes, and in his later years he was a very private man. He was a man who appears to have fallen in love with obscurity. Perhaps even the desire for invisibility.

In 1906 Chicago he visited a pair of investors, Charles and Martha Hill. Following their accepted allegiance, he scurried off to Rockville, Maryland where he captured three others. They were the prosperous and socially influential Prescotts; Alexander Fullerton, his wife Edith Stanley Kellogg, and his widowed mother of fifty-nine, Mary Richard Hill Prescott.

The Prescotts, aside from their monied status and elevated social positions, had also a touch of Revolutionary history in their tree. Doctor Samuel Prescott, a fervid Son of Liberty, had ridden with William Dawes, a twenty-three-year-old shoemaker, and Paul Revere, the silversmith, in April 1775 to warn the countryside and Concord the British were coming. He was the only one of the trio to complete his ride. While Dawes was thrown from his mount, Revere was captured briefly, then released to walk to his freedom sans horse. Two months later in June, Colonel William Prescott fought in the bloody battle of Breed's Hill, often referred to as Bunker Hill.

Arthur Manby returned to Taos in November with sumptuous financial drafts of commitment from his latest investors, embraced in rapturous joy that all was well in this best of possible games. But as six months slid by his fresh fish became concerned and complained of his lack of performance. Besides actually dragging his feet, he had honestly hit a snag regarding the use of water from several streams as a source of irrigation for his idealized agrarian aims. The opposition came from the United States Government and an earlier treaty with Mexico in protecting the Rio Grande. Briefly and simply, Manby's irrigation plans would diminish the water-flow into the Rio in violation of the pact.

Manby took his problem to a legal firm he hired, paid for with some of his new funding, Catron and Gortner. Charles C. Catron was the twenty-seven-year-old son of Thomas Benton Catron, the lawyer who defended Arthur and Jocelyn in the Griffin murder over twenty years previous, winning their acquittal. In Gortner's closing in his summarized letter to Manby, he suggested that the grant developer persuade Prescott to use his influence in Washington, D.C.

Whether or not Arthur wrote Alexander of his plight can be but surmised; most likely he waited. To allay their anxieties he wired them to come to Taos so as to discuss the project in depth.

Only too happy to accept his invitation, the Prescotts and Hills made the journey westward and arrived in Taos in late May 1907. Arthur met their stage as it pulled up before the Columbian Hotel on the plaza. He graciously insisted they spend their stay at his adobe mansion just down the street. Glad to do so, host Manby hired a carriage and all arrived somewhat in style. With the Prescott's was their young daughter, Edith Kellogg Prescott, seventeen. She was given the nickname "Pinky" because of her bright rosy skin and golden hair.

Arthur's fancy of course missed not a beat as he laid his eyes upon the radiant young maid. Although not exactly his type, for the dusky Scotch-Mexican Terecita Ferguson, his tiny princess, more than satisfyingly touched his erotic imagination. But accommodatingly he made liberal adjustments, for after all Pinky was money-based, and beneath that bright roseate skin his sonar vision could clearly make out rich tones of Lincoln-green.

The dinner gathering was a lovely evening of food and wine and conversation, sans business, with Arthur Manby at his best as the attentive, entertaining host and raconteur. But their business conference the following day was somewhat of a flop. The main contention was that the investors had sunk a handsome chunk of cash in the Taos Valley Land Company, and for six months they had nothing to show for it. The ex-host now made several desperate suggestions and financial adjustments, but to no avail. To his grim audience he looked more like a boy in the fabled finger-in-the-dike fable, or worse yet, the picture of the top-hatted and slick snake-oil salesman standing on the back of a wagon volubly describing his miraculous elixir. Arthur watched helplessly as he tried to save his sinking ship, but all he seemed to be able to do was dog-paddle in the middle of a vast, darkening sea, bravely trying not to drown. The next day the unsatisfied Hills let their feelings be known, then departed for Chicago.

Alexander's mother was the next to abandon ship, having had enough of what she felt was a cheap circus sideshow. Smelling a rat, she departed the mansion.

But Alexander and his wife Edith stayed, mainly for their young daughter's sake, who insisted on remaining. Pinky seemed to have been quite taken with Arthur and his suave fawning. They often held hands when in each other's company, and especially as they strolled through his massive flower garden while he whispered sweet nothings into her ear, she not recognizing the serpent. Despite the disparity in their ages of thirty years, Arthur must have displayed enough of the Prince Charming to win her over. Soon there was talk of marriage, and the parents had no objections. Maybe Pinky was spoiled and used to having her way, as children of the rich often are. Or being nearly eighteen they thought she was adult enough to make her own decisions. Too, her parents may still have been blinded and magnetized by Arthur's impression of affluence, and there is an old saw about wealth attracting wealth. So within a month young Pinky, three months shy of eighteen, and Arthur, one month short of forty-eight, were wed in a church ceremony on the afternoon of 22 June 1907. Her parents then gave them their blessings and departed for Maryland. But sadly, the marriage was not a happy one, nor would it last.

Yet it was rumored that Arthur had married on the rebound, another example of his twisted temper whenever aroused or crossed. He was said to have been courting a young Taos beauty but was either rejected or lost her to a rival. In spite, he seized upon Pinky. If true, he would not have been the first, nor the last, frustrated lover to change canoes beneath a stormy moon.

When Pinky's teenaged brother visited them for a time and stayed with the Manbys, it was inferred the two "would sneak out and slip away for some good times" late at night, whatever the good times meant, probably nonsensical teenaged pranks.

An earlier visitor of Arthur's was his brother Charles' seventeen-year-old son, Bertram, from Pennsylvania. He had been sent to New Mexico in the early 1920s for his health, having a tubercular hip. He was employed for a time as a chauffeur for the heiress, Mable Dodge Stern Lujan. Bertram recalls Arthur as "a strange old man" carrying a large key ring on his belt, who would ritualistically unlock and lock doors whenever entering and exiting rooms throughout the mansion.

The Manby-Pinky coupling was indeed a stormy one, for Doctor Martin next door described her as, "a pink-nosed little rabbit mesmerized by a boa constrictor." Her occasional echoes of weeping, screams of "Mister Manby!" and slamming doors did little for the doctor to look upon the union as one made in heaven.

Nine months after their marriage, on 2 March 1908, the young bride gave birth to a girl, Alice, who was a still-born, or died shortly after. Not too long following the burial of the child, Edith fled Taos for Kiowa, Colorado. There she filed for divorce, charging "extreme and repeated acts of cruelty." It was granted her, with an added award of $1,700 on 1 June by Judge George H. Fahrion.

Judge Fahrion of Elbert County, seventy-three, married and the father of five boys and a girl, was a wealthy and politically powerful individual of the area. Whether he wittingly or unwittingly played a cameo role in setting Pinky free from a fetid alliance is another unknown in the long and twisted story of Arthur Rochford Manby.

With whom or where Pinky resided while in Kiowa is a mystery. It was said, although unsubstantiated, that she met a young man in Taos, Edward Cecil Allnutt, about two years her senior, and both were immediately attracted. He was also from her hometown of Rockville. Together they left Taos for Kiowa. Was it coincidence? Perhaps through exchanges of correspondence Edward learned of Edith's miserable circumstances, maybe too was an old flame, and voluntarily came to her rescue. Then again, he may have been strongly urged to do so by family. Whatever the case, she and Edward married soon after and lived out their lives in Rockville, Maryland. He died in 1964; she in 1969. They had two sons, Henry C. and Garfield Jackson.

Arthur was neither dismayed nor distraught over Pinky fleeing the garden. Nor did he impale himself upon the romantic sword of unrequited love. He was a more practical man than that. Pragmatic, would probably be the word. Then again, Draconian might be a better fit, since he had other plans with which he was preoccupied.

The following year of 1909 was a very active one for grant developer Manby. He was industriously hustling about from February through December creating a series of new companies, all papered firms to complete his dizzying shell game. It was an impressive edifice of collage assemblage. They finally totaled six enterprises, five actually spin-offs from the first. Number one of course was the idealized nomenclature of the Martinez Grant, The Taos Valley Land Company. Close behind were its love-children, The Taos Land Company, Colonial and Security Company, Taos Irrigation Company, Mesa Irrigation Land Company, and The Taos Valley Fruit Company. With these creations Arthur would torture his investors for a few years with the cruel and usual punishment of financial legerdemain.

The companies can be likened to a series of stepping stones placed strategically across a pond, where one could securely hop from one to the other without getting one's feet wet. So Arthur too created strategic stepping stones across his boggy investment field in order to keep his feet dry, but of course without letting his clients know of his private safety device.

He spent much of the time keeping the howling Prescotts and Hills at bay, while they still rightfully sought financial satisfaction for their investments. Manby fenced adroitly with the feints and parries of papered shuffles and camouflaged defusements which did nothing to becalm them, only to rattle them further. He was quite spry at blunting their nettlesome demands of satisfaction, and appeared to feed on the atmosphere of adversity, so shielded from reality had his touch of megalomania protected him. So ensconced in his fantasies had he become, he was oblivious to the growling rage about him.

In his systematic swindling he was fortifying and shoring up his deficient self in the only way he knew, by robbing others to nourish on the verdant food of pirated gain. He had become a junkie to embezzlement, a Dracula in the marketplace supping on his compulsory sustenance of lucre. There was no turning back for him. If he held to a motto it would have been, *Ecce me! Dirigo!:* "Here I am! I direct!"

So Arthur Manby continued directing the Hills and Prescotts in his usual cryptic and confounding manner. He deceptively shuffled deeds and properties back and forth between the half-dozen companies as a stage magician in a sleight-of-hand demonstration, transferring titles, rights and debts at the flick of a pen. He drew up three different agreements for them at three different times; assigned them various rights and interests which would supposedly net them thousands of dollars from a concocted sale of created bonds; gave them liens to acreage with odd stipulations; anything and everything that sounded promising and profitable to assuage their disquiet. But it was all smoke and mirrors, the carrot-and-stick routine, and merely a Monopoly game to him. Although they probably were no longer mesmerized by his vain bluster, more than likely they listened to anything he said in the hopes the sly serpent would give up a few bushels of Red Delicious before they lost everything. Or so they hoped. But soon even that hazy mist of optimism faded, dissolved, and melted into thin air, and in red-faced sheepishness they took their losses and accepted the truth they had been duped.

To demonstrate that Arthur never left a card in his deck unturned, two years previous, in 1907, strapped for cash, he put the touch on Jocelyn in Edgewater by selling him his shares and interests in the old mining claims on Baldy; the Fairfax, Golden Era, War Eagle and Twinn. But of course Arthur no longer owned them, having sold it (them) in 1899 for $900. Now he insisted Jocelyn return the claims in exchange for the privilege of being on the board of directors of Arthur's lately formed Colonial Bond and Security Company. But Jocelyn strongly objected, unaware he held the reins to a dead horse. So Arthur surreptitiously sweetened the pot by magnanimously claiming when the Taos Valley and Land Company shares were issued he would make out a thousand shares in Laura's name, Jocelyn's daughter. Still unhappy over what he felt unfair treatment, Jocelyn capitulated. Arthur then set the value of the retrieved bogus mining claims at $10,000 and tossed them into the ragout of companies to enrich the stew, as if to prove that green is thicker than blood.

Arthur's brother Eardley earlier met an ex-policeman outside of London, now a mechanic, who desired a change in his environment, so suggested Arthur's New Mexico grant. In early spring 1907, William Thomas Hinde arrived in Taos with his wife Mary and two-year-old daughter Doris to take up residence. Arthur was quite pleased at what he felt was the first of many future settlers to move upon his planned colony. Hinde rented a small house across the road a short distance from Manby's estate, opening a blacksmith shop around the corner from the livery stable of Long John Dunn, later the operator of a stage line and real estate business.

The following year as much as Manby busied himself with a handful of projects, he grew nervously impatient awaiting his grant hearing. He was confident he would win the pending judgment, yet in the back of his mind he knew nothing in the universe was chiseled in stone; anything could happen and often did, and he had his stressful moments. Sure enough in mid-year it did. A disgruntled investor of Denver, Golden Barrett, and others, filed suit against the Taos Valley Land Company and the Taos Land Company, labeling each a pretended corporation, and to deter both from doing business. Manby ignored the complaint and quickly left for Claremore, Oklahoma to take in the hot springs and lay low. There, he had his "attending physician" send a sworn statement that his patient was too ill to attend the May term of court. To add to Arthur's anxiety a government survey of an adjoining grant was made over a bitter protest as to boundary lines. Its outcome conflicted with the Martinez Grant boundaries, which left him further unsettled and angered, hoping it wouldn't damage or skewer his future hearing. Too, occasional would-be heirs were still showing up at the courthouse with their own Martinez Grant claims.

Returning to Taos from his therapeutic soaks, he stopped off in Elizabethtown to visit the Fergusons. The rich gold-producing Aztec Mine was recently re-opened, closed earlier because of legal quarrels. A short time later it would close again for a time because of rampant high-grading. But more important at the moment was the Mystic, opposite and west of the Aztec, and the Ajax, just south of the Mystic. Wilkerson lived solitarily at the Mystic, "working the claim," while Ferguson "toiled" at the Ajax, although both men at times worked together. Both mines were known to be light wielders of valuable ore, if not exhausted, yet the pair of laborers constantly appeared to possess an abundant supply of money. If it was high-grading the two men were into, and the suspicion was there, it was very profitable, and if it were true, no one seemed to have made an issue of it, so many others also thieving. But Manby made his own tour of the region and felt too much loose talk was made of the questionable "produce" of the two mines. He then spoke to

Ferguson about it and they decided to ship their ore to El Paso, Denver being too much a potential risk of their being exposed.

Terecita was now twenty-one. Over the years Arthur watched the young child grow into womanhood, and in his eyes she had grown more lovely and enticing than ever. There were spaces of time when they hadn't seen the other for a year or two, so busy was he promoting and traveling. Now here she was, a grown woman. Still small and petite, her maturity had enriched her more fully and added that ineffable touch of sensuousness which filled his eyes with yearning.

Manby was fifty now, yet felt timeless in her presence. The thirty years between them was but an arm-reach away as far as he was concerned; a word, a caress. That evening after supper as she and Arthur left her family to stroll along the outskirts of the dwindling village of Elizabethtown, he felt a sweet completeness in her company. Time stood still for him as if he were at the center of the universe, for his life now took on meaning and purpose. "Mi Arturo," she addressed him as they conversed. The personal sound of her "mi" burned him down to his toes, stroked his entire being.

"And I am yours, *mi princesa*," he boldly ventured. "As I hope and pray you are truly mine."

There it is, she thought. For years she knew this was coming. She sensed his attraction for her even as a young girl, but was not sure what it meant until she saw him on her fourteenth birthday, and becoming aware, wished he would say something then. Each time he left she looked forward to his return, as an orphan would her rescuer, hoping he would one day have the courage to ask her to leave with him. She could feel the searing need he had for her, and her own for him grew in proportion over the months and years. She wished desperately to escape from her poverty and squalor and the continuous moving from mining camp to mining camp, the hand-to-mouth existence day in and day out, watching her mother having to slave away; cooking, cleaning, scrubbing, mending, gardening day in and day out, and she wished for something better, to leave this peon's life of servile bondage behind her. So of course Arthur became her obsessive key to freedom. And now of a sudden Arturo made his feelings for her known. It was escape time.

"I have thought of you often, Arturo. That I must admit."

His heart pounded happily at her words. "You have preoccupied my mind and heart for years, my special one. Since you were a little girl I've looked upon you as a lovely princess."

"Yes, I know," she smiled. "But I was a princess without a prince." So now the old man wants to be my prince. Ah, men and their promises. Do they ever keep them? She hoped in her heart of hearts he was different, for she had become cynical in the ways of romance after having seen the aftermath of many a courtship by strutting roosters. Pointedly she inquired, "I understand your young bride, the pink one, left with another man. Was she so unhappy, your gringa princess?"

Taken aback he swiftly snarled, "She was no princess! She was a foolish child and I was blind not to have seen her for what she was, an immature baby!"

He snarled at the memory of Pinky, the humiliation of her up and leaving to divorce him suddenly searing him. It was embarrassing to remember he calling her his "Beautiful Sunrise" because of her rich pink complexion. How did he know she would turn out to be such a blighted light?

"Ah, mi Arturo," she replied softly. "I did not mean to anger or upset you. But I had seen her many times on the plaza and could not help but be jealous of her beauty."

"A beauty, yes, Terecita, but vain and empty and shallow. Excuse my harsh response. It was not you my anger was directed against but her, and the time I wasted on her."

But she knew he married the pink one for the money connection, and she knew more. After all, even though he was her father's partner, she was her father's confidante, and knew everything. The pilfered gold, Manby and his land-grasping and financial schemes, his growing wealth from bilking others. She was no ignorant child. But then like so many men perhaps he too likes ignorant women.

"Yes, mi Arturo, I agree. You wasted your time with her. She was *muy stupido*. Forgive my jealousy."

Mollified and warming to her words, loving the caressing manner she mouthed "Mi Arturo," he took her by the elbow to gently guide her across a wide grassy field beneath a copse of cottonwoods. The ball of crimson in the west was lower now, and splashed itself across the sky in a raging and brilliant blood-red exhibition. Under an ancient tree he stopped in the tall grass and turned to speak.

"I am so happy we could be alone tonight. To talk to you of things on my mind. About us."

Here it comes, she surmised. She had felt for years he would come to her and she waited in long patience, for this too is what she wanted. He would take her away from her dismal, dull existence, away from the muddy village of Taos, away from New Mexico to the east, away to England, to London, his home town. It would be so exciting! She was so sick of the sand and mud and horses and wagons and drabness here, and her dead-end life. Yes. He would save her, rescue her, give her rebirth. Her prince had finally arrived. He had come to deliver Cinderella's other slipper.

"What is it you would speak of, mi Arturo?"

"An opportunity, *mi princesa*. For you and I both."

Yes, she mused. An opportunity. That is what it is. She could not have said it better. More for me than for him, she sighed inwardly. At last. "An opportunity?"

"Yes. For us. You and I together!" Arthur became momentarily tongue-tied in his erotic state, a rare occasion in his life, then went on in a rush. "Oh, I want you so much, princess!" he burst. "I ache for you. I have loved you for so long!"

She stood in disbelief, in joyous astonishment. *Mi oportunidad,* she sang to herself. We maneuver about in a dance: he wants me, I want escape. A bargain for us both.

Arthur stepped forward and took her into his arms, trembling, a lover in passionate heat for his beloved, anxious to taste his sultry princess. Terecita uplifted her arms and clasped them around his neck to welcome him, and they stood body pressed against body in the soft silken night.

"Yes, mi Arturo. I will be yours. As you wish."

Mouth to mouth they glued themselves feverishly. The sun had set, and with it they sank together on the dark grassy turf, entwined in mutual anticipation.

For Terecita it was the night of nights, for to her great amazement the old man was not only thoroughly machismo, but displayed a wide variety of sexual agility and acrobatics she had hardly heard of. And, while more than ample in length and girth, "mi Arturo" thankfully wielded his tool as an instrument of pleasure, and not as a club-like weapon as did a few others she had known, being no virgin.

"O-o-o-o, mi amor! *Tu choriso es muy grande!*"

"The better to nail you with, *mi corazon,*" he grinned, missing not a stroke.

Her body and heart never appreciated more the complete attention they received that evening, and her lips were surprised for the first time at their readiness and acceptance to taste and drink the fluid of his flesh. Open and responsive, Terecita learned that night what true uninhibited pleasure was, but learned also of how dangerously jealous she could be.

Arthur also was thoroughly pleased, hoping beyond hope that she would not be another Pinky, a lovely but vapid female, a complete disappointment in the boudoir who lay like a frightened, crumpled angel, unresponsive and ignorant. But he was unreasonably unkind and impatient with the Pink one, ignoring that she was totally virginal and inexperienced in the ways of the flesh. Immediate gratification failed him there. His desire for Terecita, coupled with the craving lust for her after all these years, which seemed to compound daily in his imagination, drove him like an insatiable satyr, and for her he was at his best. He was no bedpost notcher nor hobbyist of the sheets, but more of a selective sybaritic whom only certain types of women could awake and arouse. Thankfully, princess Terecita did not disappoint nor disillusion him. Whatever else held them together, their initial evening of physical and emotional bonding became the strongest of adhesives.

Manby stayed longer than he intended, ten days, but then he hadn't anticipated his romantic fortune changing for the better so dramatically and profoundly. He took a stage to Cimarron with Terecita and booked a room at the St. James Hotel for five days. They spent all their time together, intimate as honeymooners; eating their meals at the hotel dining room, shopping occasionally, and taking unhurried afternoon wagon rides into the surrounding countryside, occasionally with a tussle in the grass. Completely enjoying each other's company, Arthur smothered her with unbridled attention.

In their room she would read his cards and palm, claiming to have learned the craft from wandering gypsies. They had kidnapped and held her prisoner for a time, she fictionally confessed. Manby found her tale entertaining, amusing her as he would a child at play. But she took her talent seriously, and when he saw her features tighten up, or her eyes turn a hard jet-black at his light mockery, he stopped.

"You have a good lifeline," she intoned, scrutinizing his palm. "As a young man in England you lost your parents. Your mother was a great loss for you, and you yet grieve her."

How in devil would she know that? Guesswork, he surmised. He was suddenly confronted by scenes of parks, trees and mountains, and saw a canvas before him as he watched his mother laying watercolors upon it. Happy days, happy times! And yes, how he did miss her still. She believed in him, made him feel worthy and loved.

At another time over his cards she said, "You were later hurt in an accident, maybe a fall, and suffered from it. Because of it, when you left for America, your brothers and sisters were not sorry to see you leave.

He felt ill-at-ease, disquieted at the revelation. There was a darkness in her presence and he wished her to desist the uncanny guesswork.

In the cards she saw dire news too, the unpleasantness of which she avoided, the fearful combinations of hearts and spades. Segments of grief. "Many hearts and spades, mi Arturo."

"Hearts and spades," he smiled, drawn more into the game than he wished. "And what does that forebode?" he asked with a weak smile.

"Love and strength: my love and your strength. Both will grow," she lied, "and your strength will protect our love."

"Ah, good news for us, princess."

"For certain," she replied. "For certain."

But as she continued reading the cards for herself whenever alone the hearts and spades continued their brutal incursions, maintained their images of disenchantment, bleakness and disaster. Now and then a club would truncheon; here and there a diamond would cut. In the middle of many a night she would lay in the darkness next to her Arturo who was deep asleep, and as she listened to his soft snoring her tears would soak her face as she silently wept in helpless grief. She was completely alone in her despair and loneliness knowing the end of paradise ahead. She was a wanderer in a cere desert, and the cards were road signs of storms, bridge washouts, floods. When Manby left the room now and then to mingle socially at the crowded bar over a brandy or two, she in her solitude found herself unable to keep her composure and would break into heavy, wracking sobs, heartbroken, moaning, "Mi Arturo! Ayie, mi Arturo!" She had already sensed his coolness and regret, could see in her miserable horizon the emptiness of his promises.

They returned to Elizabethtown where he spent his last night with the Fergusons, this time with Terecita, and in the morning he left for Taos. Suddenly abruptly impatient, he had business to attend to, he explained, and would send for her in the near future. Cinderella felt unshod.

It was not until Manby returned to the walls of his nineteen-room fortress and locked it behind him that he felt safe. He noted how he had become more and more uncomfortable the longer he remained away. The familiarity of his abode had bred security for him. But, after he and Terecita were together three, four days, something else also felt threatening. There was no doubt in his mind of his love for her; the moment they embraced beneath that starless night hardly two weeks before, he promised never to leave her. It was an emotionally-charged moment of two lovers sealing their lives together. So why after only three days in Cimarron did he begin to feel trapped and imprisoned and fearful? Was it her uncanny revelations of his early life that rattled him? No, although that in itself was surprising, even a shock. He had heard of people who could see into other's lives, a talent for clairvoyance, or something, and it never happened to him before. It gave him the feeling of being exposed, the terror of vulnerability, to be stripped to the bone and left defenseless. All that was bad enough, yet it was something else. Was it in his mind, the thing which made him want to flee her, to return to the sanctuary of his fort? Did the fall really do something to his head, damage him somewhat to where he helplessly over-reacted?

No, he writhed at the thought, which had crossed his mind

too many times over the years already. It can't really be that. But he did respond to various situations in odd ways when under the siege of stress, suddenly and blindly spewing harsh words, or lashing out extremely, like at Eardley when he visited. Then again it was often justified, like smacking editor Montaner and his crony Sanchez after their verbal insults. They sure as hell deserved it. But to flee from the arms of the woman he professed to love so much, where was the danger there? Why did he feel so pressured and insecure after their initial love pact? Why did he begin to gradually withdraw inwardly from her, ending with a strong urge to run? How could he look upon the woman he adored as an enemy?

He suddenly felt a pummeling of guilt at deserting Terecita so abruptly, so unconscionably, without at least the consideration of a lover's conference. As he again thought of her words mentioning his mother's passing he saw a canvas before him, his mother painting and humming softly in the sun, he a small child reaching up to daub at a corner of its wetness. Damp colors magically came away on his fingers and he felt excited and happy. His mother looked down with an amusing smile and wiped off his tiny hand.

"Oh, my sweet little Arthur. Already a striving artist. My little genius!"

His eyes grew moist at the scene. It was so true, he missed her profoundly. He could never abandon her. She was his very reason for living. They were a part of each other, bound together and inseparable. It was she who made him feel loved and worthy and accepted. Oh, how he still missed her! So where did that leave his princess, his Terecita? How could she ever rob him of his mother's love? Was there no place for her in his heart? Was this why he sped off, terrified of losing his first love, she becoming angry and abandoning him if supplanted by Terecita? Confused and addled, guilt seemed to be following everywhere of late. His heart, his mind, his soul, he trembled. Can I find no peace?

But before too many hours Manby got back into the swing of things. Picking up his mail at the post office he found enough to keep him busy the rest of the day. A handful of checks from investors made his heart glad, including one from the Irish woman Eardley had found for him and who had become a regular "subscriber," Margaret Higgins. This time she sent a photo: a dark-hared woman of pleasant features. Well, now, he smiled. I wonder what she might be hawking?

On 20 May 1913, Manby's long-awaited day in court finally arrived. That morning he donned his best attire and strode firmly to the courthouse, understandably apprehensive and somewhat edgy, yet ready for whatever fate deemed. The special referee, United States Surveyor General for New Mexico, Charles F. Easley, read his quite extensive historical and legal report. Following its lengthy and detailed recitation, a brief recess was ordered. When court reconvened, Presiding Judge Thomas D. Leib, unhesitatingly accepted Easley's paper for the finding of the Martinez Grant for Arthur Manby's Taos Land Company. Arthur sat both relieved and stunned. It was finally over and finally his after over twenty years! He walked home alone, still in a daze, and very, very pleased.

But now he needed more money to operate; his grant was useless without it. He found himself caught in the predicament of being land rich but cash poor. Much of it was his fault he realized, in not using at least a portion of his funds he collected over the years to improve some of it. But the money he spent was seed money, he rationalized. I'll get more! Eardley came to mind, of course.

Before a month was out his brother came through again, this time with $11,500, despite his previous note, still unpaid, for $1,000 back in 1898. It was the fact of final title which compelled Eardley to send the money. But he stonily pressed and got in exchange a mortgage on Arthur's mansion—the house, land and furniture. And at eight percent. Arthur did not hesitate.

His next move was a quick visit to Elizabethtown and the Fergusons. Namely, Terecita.

Arthur had continued more of a long distance affair with Terecita for practically three years. Although seeing her whenever he could make a swift trip to Elizabethtown, he brought her back with him perhaps a half-dozen times to Taos to stay for a week. She naturally wanted to live with him, but he pleaded business meetings, problems and trips, and that the time wasn't ripe for them as yet. Patience, my love, he would beg. Patience. At first she was flattered and smitten by his concerned attentiveness, but soon she gradually began to feel little more than a tolerated guest than his beloved. It was disconcerting for her to watch him drift from heated swain to occasional visiting bed partner, as he continuously put off their having a life together. Something was wrong and she was finally more than ready to tell him to go to hell with his empty promises. Yet every time she planned to, once in his arms she delayed her anger and impatience until the next time, and then the next. She heard of women here and there and grew inwardly furious with jealousy. It had been a month since he last saw her, and even then there was a tenseness in her all the time he stayed, three days. As he departed then, she turned to him as he mounted his horse and icily remarked, "It was so sweet of you to drop by, Señor Manby. I hope next month you can stretch your visit to four days." Without an answer he rode off, knowing she was on the brink of a volcanic eruption. But he relished no more of her verbal knife flinging, wordlessly kicking his horse into a canter. He flinched in automatic reflex as a stone bounced off his shoulder. "You goddam lying gringo!" Without acknowledging her shrieking expletive or flung missile he galloped on, eager to put distance between them. Why in hell couldn't she understand he was a busy man?

And so as Manby on this revisitation was walking his horse in the late afternoon toward the outskirts of Elizabethtown, he glanced to his right and spied in the near distance Columbus Ferguson aboard a jackass approaching from an easterly direction. He reined up and awaited him.

"Columbus," he greeted. "How be you?"

"Fine, Art, just fine. Been a tiresome week, though. Ready to toss in the towel."

"That so? And why, pray tell?"

"Well, pickins ain't so sweet as it once was, with mine owners watchin like a hawk now. Really don't blame 'em, but it sure as hell puts a crimp in my take-home pay, let me tell you. And a lotta mines are played out, too. Course the Aztec is still ripe to pilfer from. Don't know how them fools stay in business, although you gotta be careful there too."

"How is Wilkerson doing?"

"Hell, the man's an artist, I declare. If there's a nugget to be stole anywhere within a hunnert miles he'll get it, come hell or high water!" he laughed respectfully.

"Well, listen, Columbus. I think it's time you put away your pick and shovel, you coming up on your sixty-seventh birthday this next January."

"That's kind of you to observe, Art. But how in hell am I to bring in money for makin a livin?"

"To be perfectly frank, my man, I've just ridden in from Taos to give you a birthday proposition."

As they rode toward the Ferguson shack on the far side of town, Manby continued.

"Seems, Columbus, that tourist auto court in Cañon was up for sale, so I bought it. I want to give it to Terecita for you and her to run. Neither of you will get rich, but at least it'll get you off the mountain, and she'll have an easier time of it collecting rent and keeping the place up. What do you think?"

Ferguson was astounded and turned to stare at Manby, mouth agape.

"Christ, Art! You are a wonder! I don't know what to say. Really I don't."

"Just say yes, my friend."

"Then yes it is, Art. My god, that's wonderful!"

"Do you think Terecita will go for it? I know I've been a bit remiss in my attentiveness toward her, but I've been awfully busy."

"She certainly will! Or at least she'd better," he laughed. "That's really the nicest news I've had in years, Art. I thank you endlessly."

"Think nothing of it, my friend. This way Terecita will be down the road hardly a mile from me. Just a small ride away."

As the two riders cantered toward the Ferguson hovel, Terecita stepped out the door and stood waiting. Even at that distance of about one hundred yards or so, Manby could tell by her stance she was not a happy camper, for she bore a confrontational air.

"Terecita," addressed her father with a big grin as they reined up before the cabin. "I have good news for us. Especially for you."

Expressionless and in mute caution she merely asked mockingly, "Really?" She had heard those words before, not only from her father and Arthur, but many times over the years from several people who bore "surprises," and they more often than not held cold disappointment. "And what is the good news this time?" she cut, showing a grim and frothy mein.

Manby leaned over with both hands on the pommel of his saddle in a wide grin and asked quietly, "How fast can you pack, little princess?"

The deep-tunneled black of her orbs faded to light grey as she smiled in sudden glee, leaping up and down, happy as a child who just received a long awaited Christmas gift. "Really? Really?" she half-squealed, hardly believing her ears. "Really?"

Arthur triumphantly stretched out his arms and slid a foot out of his stirrup. The princess hesitated not an iota to slide her own foot into the emptied stirrup to hoist herself into her lover's waiting clasp. Her prince had returned and he was in her good graces. Again.

Arthur had calculatingly resolved this no small glitch in his romantic life by presenting symbiotically to his princess her missing slipper in the form of new living quarters. A clever merchant of the heart, it was a neat quid pro quo. Yet, unwittingly, her new home would also prove to be his future death site.

So in October 1913, the "retired" widower Columbus Ferguson, nearly sixty-seven, and his daughter Terecita, twenty-five, moved to the auto court in the small settlement of Cañon, hardly a mile west of Taos on Cañon Road. Yet the Fergusons weren't in complete needy circumstances, for Columbus carried with him a nest egg of the profits from his last shipment of ore—$1,950.

Manby next got down to business by taking a trip to Santa Fe to reel in a prospective catch. He had met Margaret Waddell the year previous in Mineral Wells, Texas. Putting on the charm then, he found her open conversation a font of information coated with liberal swatches of Lincoln green. Recently from Los Angeles, she had visited Santa Fe and was quite taken by its southwestern landscape and charm of adobied architecture. She was enthusiastically thinking of moving there to build a house and reside. Arthur couldn't have asked for a better opening, and happily told her he just happened to live a bit north, in Taos. Describing the physical immensity of his grant, and greatly magnifying his financial status and business background over succeeding dinners and wine, he coolly asked her to drop him a line when she returned to Santa Fe. He was pleased when she did, and thus his trip to Santa Fe to renew their acquaintance.

He spent the next nine months of his life as an avid shakedown suitor, and relished every moment of it, as a hunter thrills tracking down his prey. It was not a mere cat-and-mouse exercise to him, but more similar to a chess game of give-and-take, and to take more than to give. It was the dovetailing of each others needs, wishes and desires; the subtle fencing of egos and one-upmanship; the verbal wrestling and injecting at proper moments of silken ploys and gambits to draw the other in. Of course one plays to crush his opponent, but it is the joy of playing the game well that counts, and his gambits were sweetly placed.

Margaret Waddell was renting an adobe house on Canyon Road in Santa Fe, an area which years later would become a noted and colorful arty district of galleries and bars, the most well-known bistro being Claude's. On and off for years it would teem with corps of artists and pseudo-artists who preyed and profited on tasteless touristas, while the gin-mills liquified the angst-ridden souls of the aesthetically predisposed.

Arthur described his ambitious project of building a resort hotel on his land, near the plaza, something in Spanish-style architecture. Taking her to Taos he showed off his nineteen-room estate in a nonchalant manner, and where he felt the hotel should stand. After the calculated virtuoso discourse of his colorful plans, they soon became intimately connected, to the point where she commenced shelling out thousands of dollars. They soon addressed each other as "Bess" and "Rochie." Before long the smitten kitten suggested marriage, and that they construct the hotel together. Arthur demurred. Margaret threw more money into the pot. Arthur complained that he needed more funding to do the job properly, that he was in touch with his financial advisors back east, etc., etc.

Short of cash for living expenses he introduced her to an "art treasure" he volunteered to part with, regretfully of course, an oil by Hubert Van Eyck. He claimed it was a masterpiece worth $100,000, but was willing to let it go for a mere $10,000. Offering her a one-half interest in it for $500, which gave her an equity of $5,000, she gave him the money. Before long he dispatched her on a hawking tour back east with the canvas to find a buyer, starting in New Orleans, then New York.

The provenance of Hubert van Eyck's painting "St. Agnes,"

as related by Arthur to Margaret, although brief, is an interesting account in itself. Painted in about 1396, it was brought to the United States around 1910 by a "French nobleman who had mortgaged it to the Chief Justice of Minnesota." But the Frenchman was unable to recover the artwork, being soon after killed by Native Americans. The picture next turned up in the possession of a Judge Emmett of Santa Fe. Emmett then willed it to his daughter, the wife of Governor Otero. She in turn sold it to Arthur Manby.

Yet, there seems to be no "St. Agnes" by Hubert van Eyck; the name of the French nobleman is unknown; there was no "Judge Emmett" in Santa Fe at the time; and Manby moving about in the social circles of the Oteros appears specious. Aside from all this, and to give the devil his due, is there a minuscule possibility Manby may have unwittingly been in possession of an unknown piece of art, as the previous owners before him, and all had passed it on in innocent belief?

The van Eyck's, from the Netherlands, appear to have had several talented painters in the family. Hubert (c. 1380-1426), of whom almost nothing is known, was the brother of Jan, or Johannes (c. 1390-1441), the most talented and well-known of the artistic brothers, and who commanded high prices. The two are said to have sometimes shared work on the same canvas. Although Jan for a time was erroneously credited as the creator of oil painting, the medium being already in use, he did perfect a remarkable varnishing innovation in the field. One of his most admired works is the "Arnolfini Portrait" of 1434. A third brother, Lambert, is mentioned in documents, while a younger van Eyck, Barthelmy, in Southern France, is also thought to be related.

During Margaret's convenient absence on her eastern assignment, Arthur made repeated rides down Cañon Road to visit princess Terecita, but she received him with chilled reserve. For some reason Arthur either misgauged the depth of her emotional feelings for him, or did not concern himself with anything out of his egocentric sphere of interest, only that she should be deliriously happy and grateful forever with the gift of her auto court. Yet to his continued vexation his visits became more an insult to her than appreciated, and he seemingly did not understand her acrimonious slurs while he continued to monotonously enumerate the importance of his various financial contacts, male or female. It was all business, he emphasized again and again, ignoring her pique.

"Monkey business, you mean!" she snapped.

She felt as a woman scorned, and believed he was playing her false.

"Please, my love, she is nothing to me."

"You lying shit!" she pained. "Then why are you not with me more? Why am I not living with you?"

"Later, my sweetheart, later," he patiently sermonized. "As I have explained: after the grant is developed and running properly. Please, princess, please understand. In time we will be together as you wish. Forever. There is so much work to be done as yet."

More often than not he would thrust a handful of bills into her hand upon departing, hoping the green of cash would temporarily diminish the green of jealousy. Once in a while she would bury her anger and graciously allow him to taste and experience the raw pleasure of her lust, the small anchor she held over him, all that was left of their floundering relationship. But as much as he claimed he loved her their torrid couplings was now a flimsy hold, for unknown to both, her prince was slowly drifting north by northwest.

Margaret Waddell, upon her return from her unsuccessful odyssey in attempting to sell the "Van Eyck," seemed to have finally wakened from her romantic miasma, angry and embarrassed at herself for wasting her emotions and time on such a dead-end affliction. Perhaps she found the painting was a fake, or at the very least dubious, as was Arthur's affection. When she looked back she often felt as if she were in the presence of two persons. The elaborate disquisitions of his plans for the grant seemed so illusory, gauze-like and nebulous now in the light of colder examination. He talked the talk, but she was left with the feeling he never intended on developing a thing. He was so filled with contradictions and inconsistencies. Was the grant only a showcase, a Trojan horse, a lure to draw investors like a magnet so as to merely separate them from their money? Much of the time he said one thing and did another, not recalling his previous comments or plans. What in hell was the matter with him? Was he forgetful or just plain crazy? She finally understood she was nothing but a business tool in his hands, no different than an invented letterhead. In scorn she wrote an angry letter to him. She apparently touched a nerve, for he replied coldly and distantly, cleverly inverting her complaints, admonishing her for not having the talent to sell such a fine work of art. He then shunted off to Hot Springs, Arkansas, feeling the sudden need of their therapeutic hot baths, returning in December. Margaret relinquished the painting, demanded the refund of her $500, and fled to the more secure confines of Santa Fe.

But Manby continued pushing the sale of the "Van Eyck," plus another oil he purchased in London twenty years previous, the "Marriage Feast of St. Catherine." He claimed it was by Titian (c. 1488-1575), or Anthony van Dyck (c. 1599-1641), and executed around 1626. If the date were firm, it was too late for Titian, dead fifty years. Van Dyke would have been about twenty-seven. Following a detailed correspondence with the Colorado Museum of Natural History in Denver, the works were shown there for a time, and then returned. He next shipped them to Philadelphia for safe storage.

Meanwhile, Margaret Waddell was furiously busy with her own letter writing, enumerating to Arthur her acidic assessments of him and his shabby treatment of her, describing in numerous mailings what a financially and emotionally scorned woman she truly was. Finally, on 14 July 1914, she filed a breach of promise suit.

Whatever the quality of the emotional glue which held Arthur and Terecita together, it did not prevent her from marrying Isias Varos of Valdez in 1915. She was driven by a fiery retaliative wrath over Arthur's broken promises of a life together, his faithlessness and seeming indifference. Her older sister Francesca was married to Isais' brother, Abad.

It wasn't too long before Manby's lack of proper management and development of the grant finally began to catch up with him. Past loans ignored suddenly appeared over his mansion like a flock of hungry vultures ready to pounce; four thousand here, five thousand there, another six here. To him it seemed everyone unreasonably wanted what was due them immediately. His lawyers, Catron and Gortner, were also hounding him. Judge Laughlin too wanted his pound of flesh. Manby felt he was being assailed by an army of snarling enemies pounding at his gate. He managed to pay some of them off, but in months more creditors yammered for financial satisfaction. In desperation he was forced to turn to his neighbor Doc Martin. From him Manby borrowed $1,000, signing over a pair of lots with water rights and a house as collateral. But on and on it continued: a creditor would dun him and he would borrow what he could to pay the debt, using more portions of his land as security for the new loans. His IOUs were wild wolves chewing and devouring the massive rug of his acreage, and he alarmingly watched the carpet grow smaller with each new bite. He felt more helpless as the days and nights slipped by, and only his princess, whom he still rode out to visit, gave him peace of mind. She sensed something was wrong as he mentally stumbled and fumbled about, as he clung to her desperately. She had become his buoy in a choppy, stormy sea, and she smiled in triumph as his growing neediness fed her leverage over him. Even though still married she calculatingly gave the old man occasional sexual embraces of solace.

"Mister Manby is still a business partner of me and my father," she would say to the often absent Isais of Arthur's visits. "He bought this court for me," she haughtily reminded him.

Princess Terecita had truly become more than a princess to Arthur now. In his slowly disintegrating mind he had gradually transformed her to where she was reborn into a necessary and cogent supporting pillar of his inner being; became the glue which adhered him to his fragile and brittle reality, a reality slowly moving through billowing clouds of fog and mist. He would retire in the dead of night with her on his mind, lovingly whispering her name to his pillow, walls, and bed. In the morning the first face he would see was hers, and he would smilingly whisper "Buenas dias, mi amor," grateful for her shimmering presence, which to him soon became as real as a rock. He was sliding away by inches, as dusk slips inch by inch into the dark of night.

So Arthur for another year staved off his creditors scratching at his door, feeding them bits of his grant when needed. But a bigger blow was yet to come, a catastrophic reversal of fortune only Macbeth could appreciate, or perhaps Timon. It were as if the Gods of Fickledom had grown weary of toying with him, for whatever reason they were dissatisfied with him in the first place, justified or not, and felt it was now time to move on to more interesting game. So they dropped the dime on him.

On the bright morning of 6 June 1916, the court in Taos ordered the Antonio Martinez Grant auctioned off to the highest bidder. Overextended in his borrowing, with the grant as his principal collateral, a legion of creditors gathered on his doorstep demanding their money. Lenders and banks, and their representative attorneys, legally made their state of affairs known to the court, and the court in turn informed Manby of the end to their patience. The grant must be placed on the public auction block to satisfy his debts. At the courthouse that morning Arthur Manby was devastated, and felt as if he were dealt a shocking blow with a two-by-four. Three years previous in this same room the land had been proclaimed all his, all his after over twenty years of scraping, scrapping and fighting for it. Now, after a measly three years of ownership, to lose it all. He naturally felt it was a dastardly plot hatched by his multitude of enemies, those greedy, conniving creditors, politicians and lawyers who were out to get him, out to steal what was rightfully his, what he had worked and slaved for for years to possess. It was a humiliating and demeaning experience for him, and worse, he knew his enemies would rejoice now. As he trod home from the plaza he felt all eyes were upon him in gleeful jubilation, spitefully celebrating his loss, happy at the turning of the tables. Laughing at his downfall. But no, he vowed. He would fight on! He would show them! Swine, is what they were! Thieving swine!

Yet, he did nothing. Perhaps he was still in shock, the news leaving him immobile. He felt like the helpless Dutch boy with his two thumbs and eight fingers thrust into the leaky dike. He compelled the court for delay; it was granted. They were in no special hurry, no date having been set for the main event as yet. In October he shot off a letter to Eardley asking for power of attorney. Although he may have accepted that the grant was no longer under his control and about to slip away from him altogether, he hoped to at least salvage what he could from the "theft" of which he felt he was the victim. He wanted to ensure not losing his home and estate of which his brother still held the mortgage. Grudgingly, and probably fortunately, Eardley succumbed to Arthur's pleas. Receiving Eardley's legal nod two weeks later, Arthur moved to successfully create the funds to pay off his sibling, over $12,000, working his magic through one of his dummy companies. His brother was one of the more fortunate, and undoubtedly sighed at his good fortune. Shortly after this, through another dummy company, he sold a parcel of Eardley's land for $7,000 pocket money.

Then a bank moved in to protect a loan of theirs of over

$10,000 by persuading the court to set aside 734 acres of the grant as collateral. To Manby's loathing the 734 acres went as the debt was quickly satisfied by someone for $7,000. A bit later Doctor Martin took over the two lots and three-room house Arthur had earlier used as security for his thousand dollar loan, since Arthur failed to pay him. Next, in February 1917, in desperation he filed and obtained a court order for delay, probably hoping for a miracle. But his fate had run out its string, and four months later, on 5 June, at ten in the morning, the inevitable occasion occurred at the Taos Courthouse, the public auction of the Martinez Grant.

Arthur had used four of his dummy companies with which to manipulate and move his funds, stocks, shares and securities (imagined and real) to and fro; the Colonial Bond and Security Company, Taos Valley Land Company, Taos Land Company and Taos Irrigation Company. As proceedings went forward he shuffled his four property deeds assiduously as possible, dealing his own version of the "magic" card scam, Three-Card Monte, which in Britain is appropriately called, Find the Lady. Real estate to Manby had always been more legerdemain than magic, and since from his perspective real estate and gambling shared the same milieu (although he never gambled), he found himself in comfortable company. As a result everyone, including the clawing attorneys, was left confused, befuddled and completely asea as to his quasi-legal business structure, transfers and dealings. It was a web within a web within a web. Yet alas, it still did not save him.

While the incomprehensible, jungly structure of his companies were akin to a mind-boggling mosaic of mismatched maps, they only delayed the inevitable as creditor after creditor by the dozens made their claims known. Although his delaying tactics hardly slowed down the attacking financial invaders, he was at least successful in that many of his collectors received merely percentages of pounds of flesh from him. Even the Hills made a claim, as did his ex-wife Pinky. While the original alimony owed Pinky was in the neighborhood of $1,700, her attorney asked for $1,500 plus eight per cent interest. She got $900. Whether Arthur haggled over it, or it somehow worked in his favor, who knows? Either way, it was bargain day for Manby at the Martinez plantation.

When it was all over Arthur was left with twenty-three acres and his mansion, back to square one. Well, at least this was his, free and clear. It had been quite a ride, and he probably sat in his roomy hacienda staring out the window sipping his tea wondering where in hell it all went, and why? His dream of a vast empire was no more. The roller-coaster had ended. It was now a visited fantasy in his mind at best, to slowly dissolve into a disjointed memory in the days ahead. He was busted, broke, left empty-handed.

Six months after the courthouse auction and the bill collectors' holiday, on a late, cold December afternoon, Mabel Ganson Evans Dodge Sterne, forty, the assertive New York heiress and patron of the arts, arrived in Taos from New York with her third husband, Latvian painter-sculptor Maurice Sterne, forty-one, and her seventeen-year-old son, John Ganson Evans. Before leaving New York a friend told her to be sure to see Taos, and now here she was. They arrived on a Sunday in a hired chauffeured Ford after a grueling seventy-five mile day-long drive from Santa Fe along a narrow dirt road, at times over frozen ruts. It was a gelid evening about six-thirty, and the winter sun had set a few hours previous when they pulled up before the Columbian Hotel on the dark, unlighted plaza, where they rented a room with meals for a dollar and a half. Over their soup Mabel questioned the hostess about home rentals. She knew of none, but suggested she see the "Doctor," that he might know. Maurice tried to dissuade her, it being so late, and he not being interested in living in Taos, anyway. But after supper she wasted absolutely no time, and ignored her husband's attempts to blunt her. At the door the hostess pointed the way into the night toward Doctor Martin's. With her son and grumpy husband in tow she sought out the office in the thick darkness, their only illumination being Maurice's flashlight.

Shuffling through the night they finally came to the doctor's house and office north of the plaza. Below a sign at the door that read "Dr. Martin," was a bell which Mabel rang constantly. A light from within came on and they were admitted into an ice-cold room by a woman who told them to wait. Moments later the doctor entered, a tall, middle-aged man with grey hair standing on end and pink cheeks. His small green eyes seemed shrewd and lively. He was collarless, wore a checkered suit that was spotted, and had a paunch. He looked them over a moment, then asked, "Well?"

Mabel explained they wanted to rent a house for the winter.

After some mundane conversation, Martin said, "Well, I'll tell you. There's an old fellow lives next to me here. He has a big house; he might rent you part of it. He's cranky as the devil, but you might persuade him—savvy? You go and see him in the morning—you'd never get him to open the door at night. Tell him I sent you, get me? Maybe he'll take you and maybe he won't. He don't have to. He's got plenty of money. But he's the only one I can think of. Name's Manby."

Outside, they stood a moment in the dark as Martin held his lamp in their faces. He then lowered his voice and said, "He's a goddamned Englishman, savvy? And a regular crook. He don't speak to anybody in the place except me, and nobody speaks to him. But if you want rooms, he's got 'em—if you can make 'em give them to you. You tell him I sent you, get me?"

Back to the hotel they returned.

Next morning after breakfast, Mabel, with the two men in tow, trod to Manby's many-roomed mansion next to Doctor Martin's. A metal sign nailed to the adobe wall next to the door spoke of some land company in Taos Valley. Ringing the bell several times brought quick footsteps to the door. It opened cautiously to reveal an old, heavy, unshaved face with eyes red-rimmed and bloodshot, glowering.

Mabel asked timidly, "Are you Mr. Manby? Dr. Martin sent us to you."

"Oh, he did, did he?"

Gruff and rude as he was, Mabel picked up an unexpectedly cultivated accent; it was surprisingly pleasant to hear.

"Mr. Manby, we are looking for a house to rent. Will you rent yours?"

He opened the door and said, "Come inside." She saw he was dressed in the dirtiest clothes she had ever seen on anyone. Filthy riding trousers and an old gray flannel shirt with a frayed waistcoat under it. His thick neck joined his heavy shoulders like a bull.

In the interim of perhaps an hour, Arthur gave them a rambling tour of the house as all chatted back-and-forth lightly. The artist in Maurice admired some small watercolors of English scenes excellently done, and Arthur agreed with Maurice as to their quality, adding proudly that they were products of his mother.

Mabel saw the upkeep of the house was dreadful, with neglect, decay and dust throughout. Yet she prodded him several times of her desire to rent a collection of rooms.

"Well," Manby finally spoke agreeably. "I would have to have seventy-five dollars a month, and for not less than six months. And seventy-five in advance."

Mabel accepted immediately, stating they would return and move in on the first of January and remain through August.

Before departing, Doctor Martin's name came up in a casual aside.

"Oh, Doc? Doc's all right in his way, but I wouldn't say he has an intelligence, exactly! Give Doc a bottle of whiskey and he'll give you some tall stories. But of course one can't discuss anything significant with him. Besides, he's a damned liar, a low-life, vulgar rascal. I could tell you some stories about him!"

Mabel returned with her son in January to reside at the

Manby mansion until September. Her husband followed shortly, occupied with packing his paints and effects.

In her several bios Mabel didn't dwell much over her association with Arthur Manby, land baron turned landlord, except in peripheral observations or brief assessments. But when she did, she wielded a penetrating and keen quill. Mainly, his frowzy physical appearance and personal dishevelment repelled her, as did his harsh attitude toward the Native Puebloan, as well as his biting sarcasm toward the human race in general. He was too much the negative misogamist for her positive, driving, controlling persona, and while Arthur kept mostly to himself, to her surprise he did have stimulating, intelligent discussions with several of her guests. Often she saw him puttering in his garden as weather permitted, especially after spring returned when he kept busy constantly digging, planting and pruning. But she was particularly taken by his voice, its British accent and soft modulated quality, of which she never tired commenting upon. Too, both being well-read, cultured, and erudite, they engaged in enough conversations to enjoy displaying their opinions and thoughts on a myriad of subjects, not only to draw each other out but to display their own minds, as intellectuals are wont to do. While Manby never took to Maurice, having an unexplained suspicion of him, he and Mabel often walked and talked throughout Arthur's spacious garden. They several times took his horses on long rides through "his" Martinez Grant—now mainly lost, of course— and he would describe to her on and on of his plans for the property, his dreams of the future. Was he aware it was now something of the past, as he talked on visually painting his grand boulevard which would encircle the entire acreage; the communities, businesses, Taos hotel and hot springs? Or was he back in the old role of setting her up so as to eventually put the touch on her? She wasn't exactly sure what to make of his wide-eyed, elaborate exuberance which sometimes unnerved her, so let him drone on and on, a doddering ancient with vibrant visions of some distant El Dorado only his eyes could embrace. She actually thought him mad.

Mabel in her book speaks of "Pinky as the third of Manby's wives." Was it true, or was she unknowingly passing on another rumor circulated at Arthur's expense? Mabel also claims Pinky "had escaped with the barber," which solidly eliminates the heiress as an ironclad source of information, Pinky having fled Taos as earlier described with a family friend whom she later married. If Manby did marry twice before, which is highly unlikely, the town being too small to hide a wife or two, unless he married secretly out of town, and being secretive, concealed them for his own personal reasons, perhaps they'll turn up in the future—unless of course the other "wives" actually turn out to be Margaret Higgins and Margaret Waddell, a pair of females whom he did not marry, but fleecily separated from their money.

One day in March, Mabel heard a verbal commotion from the front lawn by the fence and went to investigate. She saw Manby sprawled on the ground while her new cook, a German, William von Seebach, was standing over him. World War I was still being fought with Germany, and it seems Arthur, the rigid Anglophile, carried his patriotic fervor a notch too far. Upon von Seebach's friendly greeting of "Ja, Guten Morgan," Manby instantly retorted, "Don't speak to me, you goddamned Hun!" The result was an immediate explosive reaction from the cook which left Arthur prone on the lawn.

All in all Arthur and Mabel's association appeared to have survived satisfactorily, probably made tolerable through equal necessity; she needing a temporary residence, and he welcoming the rental income. In August 1918, Mabel and her son moved into her newly constructed home not a mile from the Manby Mansion. Highly dissatisfied with her marriage, she had become months previous romantically captivated with Native Puebloan Tony Lujan (Red Willow). An angry Maurice returned to New York and was divorced by Mabel. Tony and Mabel married in 1923.

With her new spouse in tow, Mabel marched ever more determinedly to her own drum, becoming a demandingly forceful and overtly intrusive hostess-patron in the lives of many of her puzzled creative guests. As a result, over the years she left a trail of both faithful adherents and rabid detractors. Her passionate embrace of the metaphysical, and her idealized attempt to connect with the Native aborigine of the southwest, may have been an attempt to create a needed symbolic home, a family bonding of acceptance. An only offspring and product of an extremely dysfunctional setting, of a cruelly unstable mother and unfriendly father lacking even the most primitive of parenting skills, left her emotionally adrift. Embezzled of her childhood, she surfaced the power-loving, bulldozing navigator of her long life's journey of eighty-three years.

Arthur Manby continued on in the way he knew best, wrapping his home and nineteen rooms tightly around him to protect him from his growing armies of enemies, imagined and real, and seeking ways and means of gathering funds with which to repurchase and reclaim his lost grant. He still had the two paintings he wished to find a buyer for, the "St. Agnes" and "The Marriage of St. Catherine," so he pushed them with renewed vigor, especially after a friend in Philadelphia asked an art expert acquaintance, Professor Pasquale Farina, to examine them. The expert, ignoring the "St. Agnes," came to the conclusion the "St. Catherine" was an original by Van Dyck. A happy Manby was then referred by his friend to contact Dr. Victor Copse Thorne of New York, a wealthy man of a wealthy family. Arthur, excited at the possibilities of a sale, and the connection to a bountiful source of money, quickly began a letter-writing campaign to his hoped soon-to-be patron.

It was true, Dr. Thorne was rich. Richer than rich. He also belonged to the exclusive Jekyll Island Club. Fifteen-mile Jekyll Island was located off the coast of Georgia and owned by J.P. Morgan.

The social clique was organized in 1888 as a fraternal playground for the upper-monied class of America. Millionaires such as Astor, Goodyear, Gould, Morgan, Pulitzer, Rockefeller and Vanderbilt, to name a few, were on its roster. Recreations such as picnicking to hunting, and croquet to golf were available, with many miles of endless pristine beaches for swimming and yachting. Many built homes and mansions on the island. Sumptuous parties and dinners, as all meals, were catered by a full staff. It was said that one-fourth of the world's wealth at the time were concentrated throughout the membership.

More sedate activities were occasional business gatherings held in desired privacy. The most historically important of them was the secret meeting of 22 November 1910. A group of six wealthy bankers and a Republican senator from Rhode Island, Nelson Aldrich, met to organize a financial cartel. After seven days, the cabal, led by Paul Warburg, representing the Rothschilds of Europe, emerged with a plan. Thomas Woodrow Wilson, the newly elected President, as one of his first acts, signed it into law in 1913. It was called the Federal Reserve System, a successfully powerful and economically controlling edict which gave the money changers of the country carte blanche at the nation's monetary trough. Although knowing full well what he did, Wilson whined martyr-like from the wings of his shabby stage, "I unwittingly ruined my country."

And so with great and eager excitement, Arthur Rochford Manby commenced a running correspondence with Dr. Thorne with the aim of winning his mind and heart, starting with the description of his classic art work, "St. Catherine," executed, he crowed, by no less a painter than Anthony Van Dyck. He wrote as a feverish fan attempting to impress an idol. Breathlessly extolling the oil and echoing his examiner Farina's enthusiasm over it, Manby in addition tossed in his estimate of its worth as nearly $394,000. In a later communication Arthur set its value at $125,000, but that he would let it go for $75,000, or probably even $50,000, having a need of funds. He offered Thorne ten or fifteen percent commission if he could find a buyer. But he didn't stop there.

He went on and on, in letter after letter, practically laying out his business ambitions for the doctor, with the aim of drawing him in as an investor. He described the Martinez Grant, and how he still claimed 18,000 acres of the Los Luceros Grant, in phrases of elaborate potential plans they could share in; raising and grazing thousands of sheep, the possibilities of $7 million in wealth from a copper deposit, the cutting of thousands of feet of lumber, his hot springs which he wanted to fully develop into a spa resort. He piled on words and pages describing finances and acreage and funding as if they were already partners, and all he needed was the doctor's financial approval. How Thorne received the voluminous litany is unknown, but he did agree to drop into Philadelphia to have a look at the "St. Catherine," where it was kept in a vault.

Yet Doctor Thorne, although saying nothing at the time, had not much interest in any of Arthur's investment schemes, for he had enough to keep himself busy minding his own wallet. In fact, some years previous, upon his father's death, he and his brother Brink were left with an inheritance of around $11 million. But the doctor and his wife did make a trip to Denver to one of his branch offices of his Radium Company to check on his holdings there, and let Manby know he would drop down to Taos for a visit. The news left Arthur ecstatic, and he felt his life about to take a turn into the sun after his late drab and cloudy times.

The Thornes took a room for an overnight stay at the Columbian Hotel. Manby met them and off they went to his hot springs where he lauded the water as radioactive, hoping the doctor would leap at the news. But Thorne remained aloof to Arthur's business overtures and patter, not leaping at the offered opportunities in copper, sheep or timber. Or his spa. Perhaps he merely visited out of curiosity. Before leaving, the doctor mentioned as an aside that he had not found a buyer for the Van Dyck. The Thornes then departed for Denver and their return east. The three would never meet again, except through postal exchanges.

Meanwhile in January 1921, the other shoe fell and Arthur was once again thrust into the cold, but this time for certain, as the grant went into the coffers of a more ambitious and money yielding individual and his newly formed company. It ended forever any chance of Arthur ever retrieving his now somewhat tarnished grail. He withdrew further into self-exile within the confines of his nineteen rambling rooms to brood and mull on his loss, curse his fate, and make his therapeutic trips to his princess Terecita. At least she was there for him, to soothe and coddle him, encourage him away from the dark ocean of his growing disappointment, anger and darkness. They were after him again, he could hear them. But she would help him.

On the evening of 28 September 1921, Bill Wilkerson dropped in on the Fergusons in Cañon. He was their old mining partner returned from El Paso after dispensing a load of ore, probably the trio's last. He proudly sported a new suit, hat and shoes. He also had with him $78,000, and a fool was about to be separated from his money. And his head. Exactly in that order. No one seems to know precisely what had taken place, but detective William Martin, assigned to the case after the discovery of Bill's body, tried his best to unravel all the knots and loose ends of this event also, and identify all the headless bodies.

The bloody scenario would return to haunt Manby over the ensuing years, torture his sleep and waking hours both, especially as he became more enfeebled and unreliable in his last days. Guilty conscious? Mental deterioration? Or both?

Yet for the moment Arthur Manby trundled on. Disgruntled per usual, he at least had some pocket change to see him through for a time, if the $78,000 was divided equally by three, $26,000 for each. For a short moment's work it was not bad at all. Really. And tax free.

Then Arthur's old albatross, Margaret Waddell, appeared again, as she had now and then in an attempt to settle her judgment against him, her breach of promise suit and money owed her she had put out. But her old suitor was still his wily self, continuously one step ahead of her legally. Or better yet, demi-legally. The suit was for $16,700, but was soon reduced to $7,000. Still, she failed to collect a dime.

Manby now turned again his attention to his old pet fantasy project of old, the development of his spa. After twenty years of dreaming and scheming over it, it was still there, undeveloped, but bright and shiny before his far-seeing eyes. He could not resist. So he sat down and composed a somewhat visionary treatise on this, his favorite subject. He wrote of its physical properties and included a chemical analysis chart and report of water samples; told of the spring's marvelous and miraculous cures; enclosed his personal sketches of the rocks with Indian hieroglyphs and flowing water; described a collection of ancient romantic legends of the Aztecs, the Pueblos, the Zuñis; and name-dropped Montezuma of the Aztecs, and Malinche, the Zuñi maiden-Queen.

With this steaming pot of bouillabaisse, or more correctly, fishy *olla podrida* of cobbled history and contemporary sales pitch, Arthur delightfully bundled up the pages and sent them eastward, to fly and soar as good news, he believed, to reach and embed itself into Doctor Victor Thorne's soul and heart. Or more realistically, his wallet. Like a good scout, Arthur never gave up.

For the good part of a year Manby wrote weekly to Victor Thorne, unreeling plan after plan, and scheme after scheme, in an effort to entice him to invest in his various ventures; his herds of sheep, tons of lumber and mountains of gold, and of course, his spa. The "St. Catherine" came up again, and this time Arthur boldly asked for a few thousand dollars toward it, but Thorne wisely and gently advised him to look to his own bank. Undeterred, blindly confident, resolutely focused, Arthur continued on, jay-walking, crossing against both the yellow lights and the red, ignoring traffic, a risk-taking pedestrian hopping and jockeying between cars, wanting but one thing, to get across that street. But the Avenue of Thorne deftly parried and blocked Manby's endless overtures like the natural pro he was, probably enjoying the contest, seeing it as a drill, a good practice in which to keep in shape, while undoubtedly looking upon Arthur (in between oh, hums), as maybe a better-than-average con.

At the end of the year Manby attempted a new tack, actually a variation on the theme of art, and the masterworks he claimed he possessed. He wrote that Professor Farina believed now that the "St. Agnes" had been painted by Rembrandt's best student, Govert Flinck. It was true, Flinck was the best of the lot who studied under the Dutch master, and he turned out some respectful works during his own lifetime. Arthur said it would cost him the sum of $240 for the restoration of both the "St. Catherine" and the "St. Agnes", and hoped the good doctor could send him the fee so as to do so. But Thorne Avenue was still blocked against crossing for some unexplained reason, and this time the doctor didn't even consider an answer to his request. Manby could only stand in mid-traffic, embarrassed and befuddled. All his schemes and dreams which depended upon Thorne came to naught, and he was left unrealized and empty.

It is a complete puzzlement and bafflement wherever in the world Arthur Manby got the inspiration for his next brainstorm (and last), of separating people from their wealth. It was so foreign from his usual m.o., and so alien from his normal style, that one still scratches one's head over it. Was it really his concept, this "secret service" organization, which was nothing more than a Disneyland cloak-and-dagger front for wholesale extortion through fear and intimidation? Could it not possibly have come from Terecita or

Columbus as a half-baked idea, then taken and given it form and shape in Arthur's hands? Well, maybe, but highly unlikely. Not that the Fergusons were incapable of such intricate mental plotting. But they were more into solid, everyday thievery and murder, Columbus earlier on having had a hand assisting Wilkerson in dispatching a body or two in the mountains, including partner Stone. So Manby, this failed land baron and one-time landlord, this schemer and semi-successful confidence man, may have finally gone around the bend in his desperation in a search for a solution to his financial insecurity, and somewhere came across a questionable, if not inane, idea of a secret society, which actually echoed the crude extortion techniques of the Black Hand thugs in New York City. The New Yorkers called it "protection." Perhaps Arthur discovered an article describing the Black Hand letters sent as death threats, and in his semi-enlightened state carried it a step further to form his "United States Secret and Civil Society, Self-Supporting Branch: Grand House Service Number 10." The grandiose title may have been Arthur's lame attempt at giving his fraternity the decorous aura of an English private club.

Whatever the case, the "agents" stealthily crept forward insidiously to blanket the town with dark rumors of the presence of the organization, fingering monied individuals here and there to "join" their society. Or else. With continued menacing tactics, enough new members took oaths of allegiance and paid their dues to give the plotters courage to move on to others as the weeks and months slipped by. They fortified their dread reputation with flashing light signals in the foothills in the dead of night; assigned members strange missions; and Manby at times flew the flag at his house at half-mast, a puzzlement to locals, but believed to have arcane meaning to members. It was all reminiscent of young boys' clubs and child's play which so many of the puerile set and teens go through, a sort of a rite-of-passage-on-the-way-to-manhood thing. But of course these adult adolescents were not toying about. They brought with them to their malicious club bloody purpose and serious aim, and for a time believed they were the genuine thing, an omnipotent force to be reckoned with, and not merely a collection of low thieves playing boogeyman to scare people out of their wits and wallets. Soon, a subtle effluvia of trepidation blanketed the town to become a part of the local atmosphere. Fear and suspicion worked in the Society's favor. It embraced the area as a clinging miasmic shroud. Dread fear, a freezing factor which paralyzes, can leave one helpless and at the mercy of the unkind dark forces of the imagination.

Arthur returned to writing Doctor Thorne after several months, perhaps needing in some twisted way someone to boast to, and who else but to a rich man who had spurned his money-making plots and schemes which would have brought them millions, to advertise his new importance in the wild-wild west? He described his late activities as if he were the bodacious leader of a revolutionary army, a Lenin of the west at the head of his troops fighting off bands of gunmen day after day. The doctor must have rolled his eyes, wondering what in the world Arthur was smoking, drinking or chewing, or maybe all three. The rambling letter made little sense, and read like the first or second draft of a bad movie scenario.

A few of the big financial losers who added to the Society's treasury appears to have been merchant Alvin Burch, his son Clyde, and his son-in-law, Cecil Ross, possibly to the tune of thousands. Before it was over, Alvin would be left bankrupt. Cecil, suspecting his father-in-law was being hoodwinked, intentionally joined the Society to collect proof and ferret out the guilty. But before long he realized he was in deep stuff, and spying on the spies quickly lost its romance and motivation. Letting them know he had decided to resign, he was told in no gentle terms by Carmen Duran that nobody leaves once they join.

One day Manby received a letter from Thorne. The doctor

had found a pair of IOUs of Arthur's for $500 each and requested payment. Manby replied in a circuitous manner, disjointed as before, as if Thorne had pushed a replay button, and Arthur went on about a horrible running fight reflecting a small civil war, and he was now evading gunmen. The words were short on clarity but long on fantasy. In six months the doctor wrote again, but still no results, only a story from Arthur that he had some swamp land in the Ozarks where he planned to trap muskrats for pelts. Arthur next wrote Thorne that he would give him the Van Dyck, worth $50,000, for $5,000 to settle his $1,000 debt. A strange trade-off, indeed.

In the final years of Arthur Manby's life he was slowly and inevitably melting away mentally. Whatever damage he sustained from his serious concussion after his fall from that second-story balcony as a twenty-year-old, it was now accompanied and compounded by the illness Doctor Thomas Martin had been treating him for of late, paresis of the brain, the last stage of syphilis. The disease was eating away his mind, slowly taking away what was left of his sanity and intelligence. His moments of lucidity were gradually shutting down and he was turning into a malfunctioned robot, a short-circuited cyborg. His decisions, while earlier erratic, were now nearing incomprehensibility. He was month by month coming apart, imploding inch by inch, while not realizing himself how close on the road to madness he was journeying. Sadly, he was now mainly looked upon as an eccentric, a cranky old man. No one realized how ill he actually was. More or less an isolationist most of his adult life, he was now a pariah, a near outcast, and avoided as much as possible. Having alienated so many, he was now divorced from the general population. He was truly alone. He had only his princess to cling to, and she now had her own agenda.

The Society galumphed along, collecting members and squeezing what they could from them, sometimes cash, other times property, but slowly falling apart. Lawsuits between Terecita and

Burch took up some space and time, with Arthur becoming more quarrelsome and shorter tempered. Arthur's authority and leadership of their fraternity was gradually slipping away from him, little by little going to Terecita and her new lover, Carmen Duran. Arthur and Thorne reconnected again, Manby borrowing another $5,000. Before long Manby ended up signing over to the doctor practically everything he owned as security for his indebtedness.

In about 1923, Columbus Ferguson, seventy-five, was committed to an insane asylum where he spent two years. Released in 1925, he spent the remaining years of his life living with his daughter, Terecita. He died in Taos on 3 January 1927.

Sometime shortly after 1920, Terecita and Isais Varos were divorced, leaving her custody of their two children, Juanita (Jennie) born in 1915, and Columbus, born in 1918. The father of her three following children, May, born in 1922; Lloyd, born in 1927; and Cristopher, born in 1929, is unknown, although Manby's name has been bandied about by local lore.

For the last three years Carmen Duran was living with Terecita at the auto court, as the pair, to Arthur's discontent, gradually dominated the running of the Society. To add more severely to his dissatisfaction of course, was her abandoning Arthur for a new and younger lover. Yet she affirmed continuously her feelings for him, trying to mollify him in any way she could, short of physical contact, aware of his illness, in order to maintain a semblance of cohesion between the three of them for the sake of holding the Society together. But at times it was difficult for Manby to keep a rein on his jealousy, and he and Carmen would have a few sharp words when they would visit Arthur. Much as his princess would attempt to play the arbitrator, it was not a pleasant predicament. It had the makings of a future clash, if not explosion. Their last words gave evidence of it not a few days before when Terecita, Carmen, and her nephew, her brother's son, George, dropped in one afternoon. As could be predicted, the two got their backs up and crossed verbal swords over practically nothing.

"Aw, go screw yerself, Arthur!" cursed Carmen.

"Well, listen to me, you filthy blackguard!" retorted Manby. "I never want you in this house again! Get to hell out of here right now and never show your face here forevermore!"

"Suits me, you crazy limey!" he roiled. "And keep the hell away from the auto court and Terecita! You pester her any more and I'll kill you, understand? Understand?!"

"You'll do no such thing, you young fool! I have as much right to visit her as long as I wish! If she does not desire my company she'll say so!"

"We'll see about that, god damn you!"

"Please, you two," injected the princess. "Stop your fighting right now!"

The trio quickly drove off, leaving suspended in the air behind them a cloud of black fury.

Arthur, several days later, frantically missing his princess, and needing soothing balm for his troubled heart, decided to ride out for a visit, despite the heated quarrel. That early afternoon of Sunday, 30 June 1929, blacksmith Hinde and Doc Martin saw him ride off astride his horse from his many-roomed mansion, which of course he locked behind him.

re me, A.R.Manby, who after being
he is the defendant named in the
and understands the same and that
wn knowledge, except as to those
and belief, and as to those matters

16 day of February, 1905.

Notary Public.

A.R. Manby's signature on his 1905 deposition.

A.R. Manby before his fireplace in the company of his mother-in-law, Edith
Stanley Kellogg Prescott (circa 1907). Photograph, Edith Kearny.

Dick Rogers. Photograph, Edith Kearny.

Jocelyn Manby home, 1911–1926, Wheat Ridge, Colorado,
now Richards-Hart estate. Photograph, J. S. Peters.

Headstone of Jocelyn and Luella Manby. Crown Hill Cemetery,
Wheat Ridge, Colorado. Photograph, J.S. Peters.

Headstone of Columbus Ferguson, father of Terecita Ferguson, Arthur Manby's
last paramour, Kit Carson Cemetery, Taos, New Mexico. Photograph, J.S. Peters.

Headstone of Mabel Dodge Luhan, Kit Carson Cemetery, Taos, New Mexico.
Mabel Dodge hired Charles Manby's son, Bertram, as her chauffer for a time.
Photograph, J.S. Peters.

Margret Higgins of Ireland, an old
friend of A.R. Manby, and a heavy
stockholder in Manby's various
investment companies.
Photograph, New Mexico State
Records Center and Archives, #76729.

Entrance to the Mystic Mine. Photograph, Bill Cotter at billcotter.com

Mystic Mine entrance and shed. Photograph, Bill Cotter at billcotter.com

Looking down upon the Mystic Mine entrance.
Photograph, Bill Cotter at billcotter.com

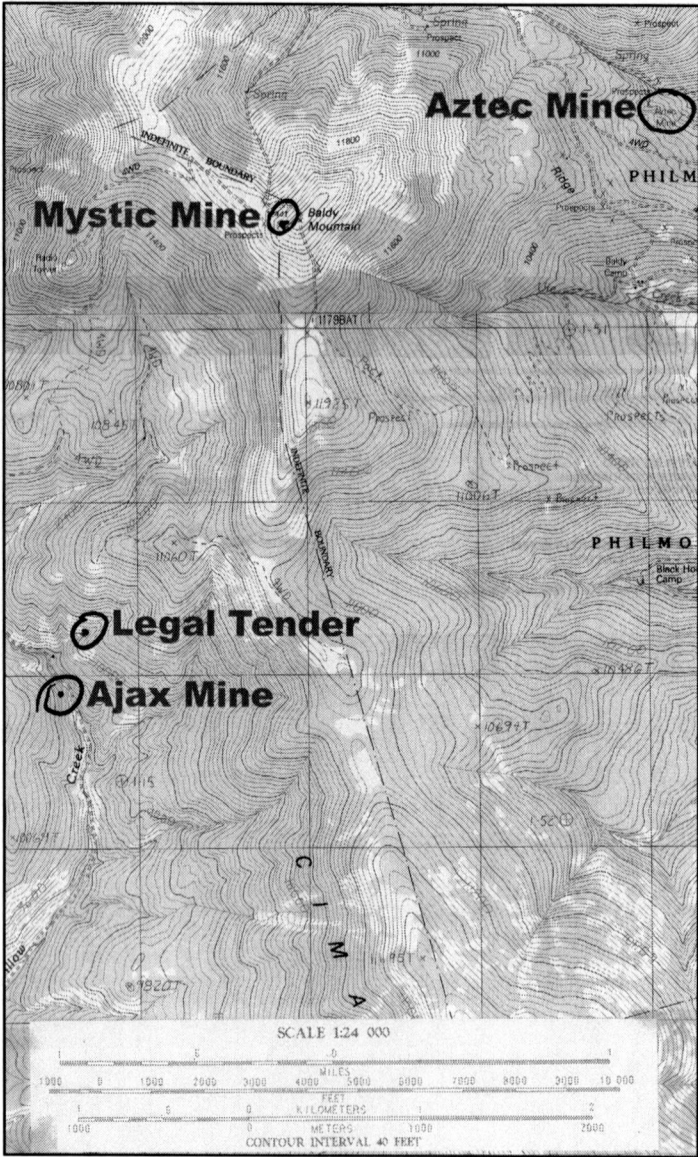

Geological survey map of Manby and Partners' operating arena.
Web: Topozone

Entry diagram of Manby mansion, Santa Fe New Mexican, March 13, 1930.

Last photograph of A.R. Manby.
Photograph, New Mexico State Records Center and Archives, #76730.

Photograph believed to be of Columbus Ferguson.
Photograph, New Mexico State Records Center and Archives, #76732.

"Old Man Stone", thought to be A.R. Manby's partner in 1893.
Photograph, New Mexico State Records Center and Archives, #76731.

A.R. Manby's barns and stock.
Photograph, New Mexico State Records Center and Archives, #76735.

Detective H.D. Martin's photograph of John Strongberg's shack, 150 yards
from Manby's grave. Land given to Strongberg by Terecita Ferguson.
Photograph, New Mexico State Records Center and Archives, #76734.

Detective H.D. Martin's photograph of W.H. Robert's re-examination and autopsy of A.R. Manby, 21 August 1929, assisted by Dr. T.P. Martin and Dr. Fred Muller. Photograph, New Mexico State Records Center and Archives, #76733.

Headstone of A.R. Manby grave, Kit Carson Cemetery, Taos, New Mexico, with inscription: "He planted the trees in this park and along Pueblo Road," —with the help of Tony Luhan. Photograph, J.S. Peters.

Manby Family Tree, compiled by Alfred Manby, 1926

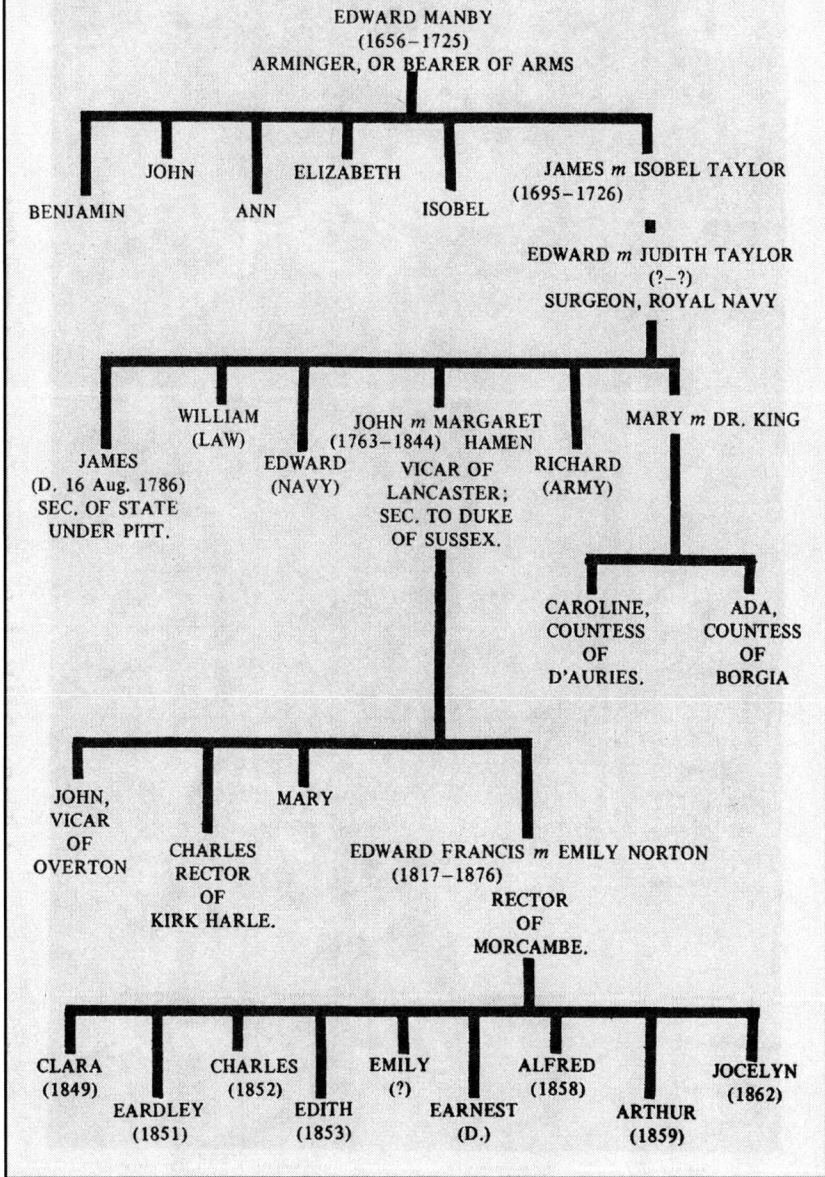

EDWARD MANBY
(1656–1725)
ARMINGER, OR BEARER OF ARMS

BENJAMIN

JOHN

ANN

ELIZABETH

ISOBEL

JAMES *m* ISOBEL TAYLOR
(1695–1726)

EDWARD *m* JUDITH TAYLOR
(?–?)
SURGEON, ROYAL NAVY

JAMES
(D. 16 Aug. 1786)
SEC. OF STATE
UNDER PITT.

WILLIAM
(LAW)

EDWARD
(NAVY)

JOHN *m* MARGARET
(1763–1844) HAMEN
VICAR OF
LANCASTER;
SEC. TO DUKE
OF SUSSEX.

RICHARD
(ARMY)

MARY *m* DR. KING

CAROLINE,
COUNTESS
OF
D'AURIES.

ADA,
COUNTESS
OF
BORGIA

JOHN,
VICAR
OF
OVERTON

CHARLES
RECTOR
OF
KIRK HARLE.

MARY

EDWARD FRANCIS *m* EMILY NORTON
(1817–1876)
RECTOR
OF
MORCAMBE.

CLARA
(1849)

EARDLEY
(1851)

CHARLES
(1852)

EDITH
(1853)

EMILY
(?)

EARNEST
(D.)

ALFRED
(1858)

ARTHUR
(1859)

JOCELYN
(1862)

Manby Family Tree, compiled by A.R. Manby, 1926. Courtesy, Edith Kearny.

Part 3

Atropos

$\mathcal{T}$he last time Arthur Rockfort Manby was seen alive in Taos was late Sunday afternoon, 30 June 1929. Perhaps a dozen people, adults and children, saw him as he was riding along Cañon Road and Kit Carson Street heading toward home in the dusk at five-thirty. He was astride his black steed returning from a visit to Terecita's house in Cañon.

Upon approaching Ramon Garcia's abode, who was standing in his front yard, Arthur greeted him with a "good evening" and reined up a moment to chat. He told Garcia he would soon be able to repay him the fifty dollars he borrowed earlier, for he expected shortly to be receiving a large sum of money. After a few more words of conversation Garcia invited him to have dinner with him and his wife, but Manby demurred and continued home, a short distance away.

Two days later, on the early evening of 1 July, Arthur was delivered a note from Terecita saying she was ill, and asked if he would please visit her. Like a fly anxious for the web he eagerly dressed, locked up the house, saddled his mount and cantered back to Cañon. As he hied to the side of his idealized amoureuse that night he probably worried about her illness and to what degree she was incapacitated, as any man would over the woman he cared about, hoping it wasn't anything serious. He may also have had thoughts of Carmen Duran too, who was surprisingly civil to him last he saw them two days before. In a moment of clarity he realized both were insanely and insurmountably jealous over the princess. His princess. Looking back he couldn't help but smile at remembering how earlier he flew into a choler and ordered Carmen out of his house, forbidding him to ever return. Carmen did so, but retorted in parting rage that he would kill Manby if he didn't keep away from Terecita. Perhaps the young man had second thoughts for he had only kind words last he saw them. Yet, Arthur inwardly writhed over her unfaithfulness to him and his being "supplanted" by a younger rival. But deeply and obsessively needing her, he somehow blinded himself to the inevitable through some circuitous, Byzantine reasoning, as had many myopic lovers in the centuries before him and since. He knew she lied, but he shelved the thought.

"I am always yours, Arthur, my love."

My princess! Manby agonized in angst, a galloping knight delivering his heart to his beloved through the dread of night, for he had developed a dread fear of the night over the last months. He never left his house after sunset any longer, locking his fortress and all nineteen rooms around him tightly. He began sleeping in a different room each night, sometimes moving two or three times. At ten in the evening, then two in the morning he would occasionally make a shift, unlocking then locking each door behind him. As he related the story to an acquaintance or two gleefully, it was as if he were successfully outwitting a ghostly pursuer. His paranoia now gripped him as a shield, his barrier against harm, having the thought, or intuition, or just plain gut feeling someone was out to kill him. But when Terecita summoned, he instantly set aside his fears and caution, feeling safe with her. "I am always yours, Arthur." And of course his very being answered: I never want to lose you. Never.

"Never!"

But sometimes a lover's "never," which meant to him never-ending, or forever, becomes embarrassingly a brief speck in time. Like a comma. Or an ampersand. Not even a footnote.

So he galloped on through the black gloom around him despite his inner fears, delivering his heart and head to his amorata, an ancient knight-errant of seventy in desperate need of his forty-year-old princess. To his appointment with fate, or destiny, or karma or kismet. Or just plain disaster.

Two days later, about noon on the third of July, Deputy United States Marshal James Martinez arrived on a drive up from Santa Fe to serve papers on Manby concerning the renewal of a breach of promise suit. It had been legally satisfied ten years previous in Santa Fe in favor of Margaret Wadell for $12,034.13, but Arthur paid no heed to the court order. Hence, its renewal. The marshal called at the Manby residence, but the outside main door was locked and no one answered his rapping. Going to the office of Deputy Sheriff Malaquias Martinez, his brother, he explained his dilemma. Malaquias thought something unusual might be wrong, for Manby was normally seen about town at least once a day, and he hadn't made an appearance since 30 June. He suffered greatly from asthma and rheumatism, explained the deputy, and complained of a troubled heart. Curiously too, the town was already aswarm with rumors he was dead. The two lawmen left for Manby's.

According to William T. Hinde, Manby's close neighbor, around twelve-thirty that afternoon young George Ferguson, nineteen-year-old nephew of Terecita Ferguson, had for some inexplicable reason given the alarm that Manby was dead. A group of people were already gathering before the outside gate of the Manby home by the time Hinde approached the place. In the group he saw Sheriff Malaquias Martinez, Dr. T.P. Martin, M.A. Spots, Des George, Bill Jenkins, Terecita Ferguson, George Ferguson, Carmen Duran, Mrs. Felix Archuleta, John Shomberg, and a number of others.

Everyone stood before the front gate outside the wall wondering how to gain entrance. Many were nervously aware of the vicious dogs Manby was said to keep in the interior patio, and someone brought up the idea of arming themselves with clubs and guns. At that unappetizing thought much of the crowd sidled off.

Carmen Duran then dug a key out of his pocket and opened the gate. Leading the way authoritatively, he led his followers around to the back patio and unlocked the back door. Into the house they went, Duran going directly to Manby's bedroom just off the hall where his body lay upon a cot. A German police dog lay on the floor next to his master's body, the animal some time earlier a gift to Manby from Duran. Duran addressed the dog, "Here, Lobo," took him by the collar, and led him out the screen door to the patio where he chained him to a kennel. Everybody then stood staring upon the headless cadaver of Arthur Rochfort Manby.

"The place was full of blue flies and the smell was terrible," described Hinde. "Around the torso was a great number of maggots. The body was badly swollen but not decomposed. It was partly dressed. The clothes on the body consisted of heavy underwear, a red sweater, and a khaki coat. His hands, feet and sexual parts were exposed. The body was resting on its left side. The left hand was in a clutching position; the right hand resting over an army blanket. The biggest part of the blanket was hanging over the side of the cot. At first it was hard to see exactly the condition that the body was in as the maggots were thick around the neck and the body was badly swollen. I, myself, took out of Manby's pocket his watch. We took the cot with the body outside of the house. We then went inside to look for the head which we found in the room next to where the body had been discovered. The right side of the face was gone but the left side intact. We put the head on top of the torso, wrapped the body in the same manner which we had found it, with the blankets that he was lying on, and laid it in a wooden box that had been brought over by the authorities.

"In the meantime a coroner's jury was formed. Mr. D. George was foreman. The theory was advanced, at that time, that Manby died of natural causes and that the police dog found with him in his room had chewed his head off. So without any further investigation the body of A.R. Manby was taken to the back of his lot, by the side of the Kit Carson cemetery. There we dug a grave and buried him. The verdict of the coroner's jury was that Manby died of natural causes. Within an hour from the time that the body was found, a jury was formed, a verdict was rendered, a grave dug, and A.R. Manby was resting six feet underground."

To add to the gory episode, already made a touch confusing by the varied recounting, the deputy sheriff a few days later was told of some men's clothing lying by the side of the road about three miles from town, along Taos Cañon. Martinez drove out and found a pair of coveralls with one side slit from waist to ankle. Beneath them was a suit of underwear soaked with blood, as if they had been immersed in a bucket. There was also a shirt with a pair of slashes, one on the sleeve, the other on the back, and one stocking.

Three days after the discovery of the headless corpse of Arthur Manby, there occurred a bloody melee outside a bar on Cañon Road just east of Taos on Saturday night of 6 July. It was a small echo of the Manby carnage in its fury and violence, an outburst just short of death. Five men became involved in a knife fight. George Ferguson and Juan Duran stood off Dan Garcia, Tomas Rivera and Alberto Sisneros. Whether a legitimate quarrel of honor, or the result of a heavy dose of testosterone soaked in beer, or if the trio may have made mockery of how it took four "bravos" to kill off a sick old man, no one to date has yet made clear. But the Ferguson-Duran team held their own admirably. Garcia absorbed a cut across an eye, serious enough to be sent to Albuquerque to an eye specialist; Rivera was badly cut about the face; and Sisneros took a slash across his throat. Neither of the two duelists who held them off appeared to have been touched. The article in the Taos paper explained the cause of the fight was not yet known, but the case would be brought before court "as soon as Garcia and the others are able to attend."

Shortly, private detective Herman Charles "Bill" Martin of

Santa Fe was hired to investigate the Manby murder by Attorney General Miguel A. Otero Jr. A highly successful and respected private eye, the thirty-four-year-old Swiss took to the trail avidly, arriving in Taos late Tuesday morning of 9 July.

One of the high points of Martin's investigation was certainly on 21 August, when he was present at the disinterment and official autopsy of Manby's corpse. Also present was District Attorney Fred Stringfellow from Raton, Doctors Thomas Martin and Fred Muller, dentist Saca Muelas, undertaker W.H. Roberts, and blacksmith William Hinde. Following a thorough forensic examination, the cadaver was definitely identified as Arthur Rochford Manby, and with absolutely no doubt it was determined his head had been removed by a sharp instrument, and not chewed off by a starving, thirsty dog.

During the course of his investigation Martin wrote three reports, each in consecutive lengths of eleven, fourteen, and three pages. His brief three-page summary, which he labeled a "Supplemental Report," and which follows, emits the twin aromas of political foot-dragging and legal shoulder shrugging. It also exudes the faint emanation of a gumshoe who had become *persona non grata*, and had overstayed his welcome at the Taos murder-fest.

"On September 5th, 1929, I was authorized to go to Taos with Mr. Otero to continue the investigation on the Manby case. On the morning of September 6th, 1929, between the hours of 8:30 and 9:00 a.m., Mr. Otero together with Mr. Miller, his Assistant Attorney General, Mrs. M.A. Otero, Jr., and a Mr. C. Clayton, representing the Chicago Tribune, met me at Tesuque from which point we proceeded to Taos. Mr. Miller rode with me during the trip and asked me many questions regarding the Manby case. From his statements I gathered that if the doctors would corroborate my statements in the matter that it appeared reasonably certain that a murder had been committed.

"We arrived at Taos about 11:00 a.m. and stopped at the Don Fernando Hotel. About 11:30 a.m. we went to the Manby house where a very short visit was made by Mr. Otero and his party. The visit to the Manby house could hardly be called an investigation as our stay there did not exceed thirty minutes. At about 12:00 o'clock we went back to the hotel to await Mr. Stringfellow, District Attorney of the Eighth Judicial District. Mr. Stringfellow arrived about 12:30 at which time we all had lunch at the hotel. At about 1:30 p.m., Mr. Otero, Mr. Miller, Mr. Stringfellow and myself went to the county jail and in the presence of the Sheriff and Deputy Sheriff a conversation took place between the three attorneys above mentioned relative to the known facts of the case. A few questions were asked of me concerning the case. I suggested that the doctors who performed the autopsy on Manby's body should be interviewed and an affidavit obtained from them. Mr. Otero then authorized me to get in touch with Doctor Muller. Mr. Miller, Mr. Stringfellow, Mr. Clayton and myself went to Doctor Muller's office and had an interview with him. During this interview Mr. Otero was not present, but from Doctor Muller's offices, which are situated in the new Taos Bank Building, we could see Mr. Otero talking to a group of men on the plaza. After the Interview Mr. Miller, Assistant Attorney General, made the statement to the effect that if Dr. Martin's findings were the same as those of Doctor Muller that there could be little doubt as to the fact that Manby was murdered.

"We then went to Doctor Martin's office and were joined by Mr. Otero. I personally conducted the questioning of Doctor Martin regarding his findings of July 3rd, 1929, and of August 21st, 1929, being the dates when Manby's body was found and the date of the autopsy, respectively. While at Doctor Martin's office, Mr. Miller and Mr. Stringfellow discussed Doctor Martin's findings, and I have given you the questions and answers in connection with this discussion more fully in my complete report to you of my investigation. At this meeting at Doctor Martin's office both Mr. Otero and Mr. Miller and Mr. Stringfellow stated that they had obtained all the information which they desired from Doctor Martin and that they had no further questions to ask. This interview ended around 6:30 or 6:45 p.m., and we returned to the hotel where we had dinner. Later, Mr. Otero and his party returned to Santa Fe. In so far as I know and in connection with my investigation, this is the only time that Mr. Otero or any representative from his office made any attempt to investigate the Manby case on the ground. This investigation did not exceed six hours. Insofar as I know, Mr. Otero never made an investigation of the body of Manby nor did he make any request for such investigation by himself personally. Although I was at one time directly requested by Mr. Otero to proceed with my investigation, I have never been asked by him for a report of my findings or the result of my investigation, and insofar as I know, he asked none of the doctors or others who were present at the autopsy to make a written report of their findings and investigation. At the time of the discussion which took place at the county jail in Taos, I suggested that it was my belief that we had all the evidence we needed to make arrests in connection with the murder that had been committed in September of 1921, and that the same persons suspected of that murder were also the ones connected with the Manby case, or at least all the evidence pointed toward them as being the guilty parties. I was advised at that time by Otero and Stringfellow to confine my investigations to the Manby case ALONE. (Emphasis author's.)

"It is my opinion that the detailed report of my investigations, in connection with this case, will show conclusively that any statements made heretofore made by me relative to the murder of Manby are amply sustained by the findings in connection with that investigation. In this connection I would welcome a complete investigation of the facts set out in my report and in connection with my statements.

Respectfully submitted,
H. C. Martin,
Feb. 17, 1930."

Ignored, detective Bill Martin was removed from the case, and it was shut down. (Otero's comments in an interview forty years later as to why investigator Martin's reports had never been accepted or admitted as evidence were, "How could I? One can't build a case on suspicions and imaginations. They have to be substantiated. And who cares?")

Not ten days later, on the night of 26 February, the Turquoise Hill Mob struck again. In a seizure of hubris, they decided to expand their professional expertise into the field of burglary. Terecita Ferguson, Carmen Duran, and George Ferguson broke into the home of local artist John Young-Hunter, who was visiting New York at the time with his wife, Eve. The trio ransacked the home, tossing what they could onto three spread sheets, which they then tied up into three separate bundles, then fled into the night as if they were late seasonal Santa Clauses. Before leaving they set a fire hoping to obliterate the crime scene in a spectacular conflagration. But unfortunately, the caretaker noticed a trail of smoke coming from the home and ran to see an interior room afire, which he was fortunately able to extinguish.

Alas, more bad luck hectored the scurrying trio as one of the sheets developed a tear, and as they flew into what they felt was the safety of darkness, from the small rip items would fall intermittently to the ground behind them which a blind Indian tracker could follow, all the way to Terecita's house only a mile or so away in Cañon. The next morning investigators of the crime did exactly that, and at the end of the trail they found Terecita in her house industriously busy dyeing a pair of John Young-Hunter's monogrammed silk shirts. End of new career.

Before it was over, Terecita Ferguson, Carmen Duran and George Ferguson faced a duke's mixture of charges from robbery, burglary, concealing loot, to larceny and arson. Newspapers from Santa Fe to Kansas to New York had a field day of howling horse laughs between the murder of Manby and the burgled Young-Hunter home at the expense of what was perceived as New Mexico's bungling justice system, and possibly that forced a face-saving, stronger drive to convict the trio.

The trial of the tres banditos ended 21 July 1930. Terecita was handed four to six years; Carmen seven to ten. George wisely cooperated and turned state's evidence, so escaped punishment. But he and Juan Duran each were given four to six years for their illustrious victory in the knife fight the previous 6 July.

Doctor Martin's often commented-upon illness for which he was treating Manby was the last stage of tertiary syphilis, paresis. Upon its third and final visitation, the disease settles on an organ of choice; the heart, lungs, joints, etc. The choice for Arthur's spirocheted invaders was probably the cruelest of all, his brain. When and where Arthur contracted the disease is of course unknown. It could have taken place anywhere from one to twenty years previous to his murder, the third stage itself unpredictable as to its life span, while nestled and quietly pullulating in his body. Could his illness have been the reason for Pinky's daughter being a still-born in March 1908? But Pinky went on to marry and bear healthy children, with seemingly no medical complications the rest of her life. So Manby may have become initially infected only four of five years before his death, say perhaps 1924. Or 1925.

An early antidote for the disease, mercury, was used for years. In the early 1900s, Atoxyl, an arsenic compound, was developed by the Silesian, Paul Ehrich, the father of immunology. Later, in 1910, he came up with Salvarsan, or 606. Then, an improved version, neosalversan, was remarkably successful. It was not until the 1930s that penicillin became a boon to the infected.

Doctor Martin also remarked upon Manby's medicine chest overflowing with a wide variety of medications, he having become a self-appointed medicine man. By this time he of course was probably trying every concoction under the sun and moon to eradicate his affliction.

In 1920, it was discovered "that probably twelve percent of Taos Pueblo had contracted the disease." Mabel Dodge graciously leaped to their aid as she donated financially to help the medical authorities combat and eradicate the mini-plague. Possibly the driving force behind her benevolent act was that she herself had contracted the disease from her lover and future husband, the Pueblo Native, Tony Lujan, her "noble, silent red man." Lujan, being married then, may also have infected his wife Candelaria at the Pueblo. The cure at the time consisted of injections of Atoxyl once a week for eighteen months, a painful process, then being declared cured. Sadly, Mabel Dodge's own medical history is a dire portrait of a luckless female in the world of love.

Mabel's first experience with venereal disease was through

an affair with her gynecologist, Dr. John Parmenter, a prominent physician of Buffalo society, from whom she contracted gonorrea. Married at twenty-one for the first time to Karl Evans, who worked for his father's steamship company, she soon bore him a son. The day before her twenty-fifth birthday her husband died after a hunting accident. Seemingly a loveless marriage, she had turned to her doctor with whom she was in love, with the consequences of the above mentioned infection. There was also doubt as to who actually was the sire of her son, whom she named John. To dizzier spin this downward spiraling state of affairs, since the physician was married, it was thought scandalous in that Victorian milieu for a single woman to carry on a sexual liaison with a married man, so she was shipped off to Europe by her socially-concerned mother, whom Mabel believed was also bedding down their doctor.

On the boat to France she was pursued by the wealthy architect Edwin Dodge whom she married in 1905. Returning to New York in 1912, she separated from him. In 1917, she married the artist-sculptor Maurice Sterne in Peekskill, following which they moved to New Mexico. In 1918, in Taos she fell in love with Tony Lujan, and shipped Sterne off to New York, marrying Lujan in 1923. The common legacy left her by her last three husbands was the infection of syphilis from each, and the psychological weight must have been daunting.

In Arthur Manby's case, it may have been an irony how he contracted the illness. He had earlier befriended Tony Lujan, and together they would drive into the mountains to unearth the series of trees they needed to line the road from Manby's home to the Pueblo, a physically demanding task at the time of a few miles with nothing but a shovel and strong back. Arthur's tombstone in Taos bears the statement, "He planted the trees along Pueblo Road." Whomever instructed the stone cutter of the ecological deed, he had failed to complete the information (perhaps not knowing of it), and should have added "with the help of Tony Lujan." Whatever close friendship the two shared, it widened coldly after Arthur's mental state began to unravel, making him socially unfit company. The question is, suppose during their early comradery Lujan had introduced Manby to a tainted young maiden of the Pueblo, opening the way for a coital dalliance which helped spell his future doom? Was Tony unwittingly the bearer of poisoned apples to both Arthur and Mabel? This is speculation, of course, but the strong possibility is there.

Tragically, Arthur Rochford Manby at the end of his life was caught between the horns of his own personal hell of limbo and purgatory. There was no solution or salvation for him now, let alone solace, only the darkness of a diseased death at the end of his tunnel. Whatever frontal lobe damage he sustained in his fall from that balcony at twenty, which left him with symptoms of depression, irritability, paranoia and impulsiveness, it was doubled now with his tertiary illness with the added contributions of confusion, disorientation and impaired memory that gradually turned his brain into an imploding organ. And what side effects from the stockpile of "health aids" which crammed his medicine chest were compounding his already physical and mental corrosion? Was mercury poisoning also doing its slow, insidious work?

As he stumbled mentally and physically throughout his last days, he was probably unaware of his slow deterioration, erosion and decay. There was no turning back the clock for him, no readjusting his calendar, no rewriting his destiny, no stopping his racing locomotive along its roaring journey of no return, speeding thunderously to end of track. Brutal and callous as his four murderers were, they unintentionally committed an act of kindness. If there was anywhere in history a justification for euthanasia, Arthur's plight pleaded for it, for he had truly become an invalid, a puppet, the tail wagging the dog. *Fata viam invenient*: the Fates will find a way. They certainly did, and mercifully so.

During my last four months or so in Taos in 1965, I had been living at the Fiesta Motel in Cañon, about a mile east of town. It was early fall, the weather was cooling, and the leaves were subtly turning coppery. Early one morning I awoke with a start on my back. The room was pitch-black and I was immobile, paralyzed, unable to breathe. I felt a gradual, constant pressure upon me as if I were being smothered. Thinking the sheet or blanket was over my face I tried to push it away. All I could move were my arms and I flayed in alarm at empty air. I could sense the sheet was only to my waist, then realized the blanket was folded across the foot of the bed. Soon I grew frightened and knew something or someone was trying to kill me, although for a brief moment I thought it might be a nightmare. I felt the pressure atop me grow stronger, pushing down across my face and chest. Near panic now, I realized I had to fight back, and quick. I continued flaying my arms at empty air, eyes opened at nothing but inky blackness, then shouted in fear-filled anger, "Get away from me, you son of a bitch! Get the hell out of here!" My sudden rage got me breathing again, and I greedily gasped to fill my lungs over and over as I began to feel freed of the thing. In a few moments the dark in the room dissipated and I lay back heartily inhaling oxygen, exhausted, confused and still frightened.

Through the heavy drapes covering the large picture window on my right the motel's neon lights filtered through, and the room returned to its former grey softness. I looked to my left and saw again the familiar small window, half-open, with full moonlight glowing on the curtain. From outside I heard the trickling flow of the shallow stream. Previously I saw no window, no moon-reflected curtain, nor did I hear the creek. I lay drained, glad to be alive, wondering what in hell had happened?

The next night the same thing repeated itself, but this time the weight removed itself, fleeing as I fiercely cursed it again, angrily yelling, "God damn you, get away from me!" The deep blackness had once again enveloped the room, but it too remained only briefly, leaving after my heated oaths. I felt in control then, but still nervous.

On the third night it returned once more, but was weaker still. The room did not turn completely black, the presence seemingly unsure of itself. I cursed it again, and it fled. I lay grateful, hoping it was the last of my unwelcome visitor. Thankfully, it never returned.

The next afternoon I picked up a six-pack and spent a few hours talking to the manager-owner, Charlie Bach. I related to him my three nights of terror fending off something, and he was quite blase over it.

"Hell, I'm not surprised at all," he replied. "But I'm glad it happened to you and not me. There's been a lot of strange occurrences around here over the years."

"So what could it have been?"

"One thing I can tell you is that it's believed Manby was killed where your room is. Head was cut off with a sickle."

"What!? Oh, great."

"In the early nineteen hundreds these were called tourist camps and were cheap wooden structures. Terecita ran them with her father after Manby bought it for them. Infatuated, he called her his 'little princess.'"

Charlie then related some of what I already knew, having read a little of the case, and having met and talked with Terecita several times. Soon I moved down to Santa Fe, then Albuquerque, then Denver, where years later I would further research the "Manby Mystery" for this work.

Sources

BOOKS

Caffey, David L. *Frank Springer & New Mexico*. Texas A&M University Press, College Station, 2006.

Curry, George. *An Autobiography, 1861–1947*. Albuquerque, University of NEW MEXICO Press, 1958.

DeArment, Robert K. *Bat Masterson: The Man and the Legend*. Norman: University of Oklahoma Press, 1979.

Dunham, Harold Hathaway. *Government Handout*. De Capo Press, New York, 1941.

Fergusson, Erna. *Murder & Mystery in New Mexico*. Albuquerque, Armitage, 1948.

Grant, Blanche C. *When Old Trails Were New*. Sunstone Press, new edition, 2007.

Griffin, G. Edward. *The Creature from Jekyll Island*. American Media, California, 2003, Fourth edition.

Lash, Joseph P. *Eleanor and Franklin*. New York, W.W. Norton & Company, 1971.

Luhan, Mable Dodge. *Edge of Taos Desert*. University of New Mexico Press, Albuquerque, fourth printing, 1993.

Martin, Bill and Molly Radford Martin, *Bill Martin, American*. The Caxton Printers, Ltd., Caldwell, Idaho, 1959.

Miller, Nyle H., and Snell, Joseph W. *Great Gunfighters of the Kansas Cowtowns, 1867–1886*. Bison Book, 1967.

Murphy, Lawrence R. *Lucien Bonaparte Maxwell*. University of Oklahoma Press, Norman, 1983.

Pearson, Jim Berry. *A New Mexico Gold Story*. Dissertation, University of Texas, Austin, January 1955.

Rudnick, Lois Palkin. *Mabel Dodge Luhan*. University of New Mexico Press, Albuquerque, 1984.

Rudnick, Lois Palkin. "The Male-identified Woman and Other Anxieties: The Life of Mabel Dodge Luhan," pps. 116-138; *The Challenge of Feminist Biography*. Sara Alpern, Joyce Antler, Elizabeth Israels Perry and Ingrid Winter Scobbie, Editors. University of Illinois Press, 1992.

Waters, Frank. *To Possess the Land*. Chicago, The Swallow Press, 1973.

Westphall, Victor. *Thomas Benton Catron and His Era*. University of Arizona Press, Tucson, 1973.

ARTICLES

Bursey, Joseph A. "Mystery Murders Like the Wild West Days." The American Weekly, April 20, 1930.

Bursey, Joseph A. "The Manby Mystery." The Wide World Magazine, March, 1935.

Jenkins, Dr. Myra Ellen. "Arthur Rochford Manby." Denver, Westerners Brand Book, 1966.

McGaw, Bill. "Manby Murder Mystery of Taos." The Southwesterner, Aug-Sep-Oct 1963.

Nunn, A.D. "Taos Terror." True Detective, 1950.

Peters, James S. "Masterson's Militia: Company H." Old West, Fall, 1983.

Peters, James S. "Riders for the Grant." WOLA, Vol. XI, No. 2, Summer 2002.

ARCHIVES AND COLLECTIONS

Criminal Records, Colfax County Courthouse, Raton, New Mexico.

Edward L. Bartlett Papers, 1882–1903. Collection 153, correspondence, 1885, four letters. Center for Southwestern Research, University of New Mexico, Albuquerque.

Governor's Papers, Richard C. Dillon, Manby File, Folders 98 & 99. State Records Center and Archives, Santa Fe.

New Mexico Territory vs. Arthur and Jocelyn Manby, Docket no. 1110 (incomplete), State Records Center and Archives, Santa Fe.

Registry of Births, Book No. 1, Taos County Courthouse, Taos, New Mexico.

NEWSPAPERS

Raton Comet, June 6, 1883; Sep. 26, 1884; Mar. 6 1885.
Santa Fe New Mexican, Dec. 12, 1889.
Taos Cresset, Feb. 2, 1889 through Nov. 15, 1900, scattered issues.
Taos News, July 4, 11,18,25; Aug. 8, 22,1929.
Taos Recorder, 1913 through 1914, scattered issues.
Taos Valley News, Feb. 19, Mar. 5, 1910; Nov. 14, 1929 through Mar 13, 1930,
    scattered issues.

INTERVIEWS AND CONVERSATIONS

Joseph A. Bursey, Santa Fe, New Mexico.
Terecita Ferguson, Taos, New Mexico.
Dr. Myra Ellen Jenkins, Santa Fe, New Mexico.
Edith Kearney, Santa Fe, New Mexico.
Frank Waters, Taos, New Mexico.
John Yaple, Taos, New Mexico.

I especially wish to extend my thanks and appreciation to Al Regensberg, Sandra Jaramillo, Felicia Lujan, Daphne Arnaiz-DeLeon and Gail Packard of the State Records Center and Archives in Santa Fe; to Donald Burge of the Center for Southwestern Research in Albuquerque; Kyle Ayers of the University of Texas Library at Austin, Texas; and Amy Denniff of the Edgewater Public Library for their patience, time and cooperation in the furnishing of various historical documentation. Also to Monte Pruett for his research input and genealogical data. And last but not least, to Frank Waters, wherever he may be, for allowing me the use of "To Possess the Land" as a loose framework (and sometimes not too loose), for this work. Much appreciated, Frank.

Lightning Source UK Ltd.
Milton Keynes UK
UKOW05f2344211013

219514UK00006B/943/P